CONCEPTS AND INQUIRY:
The Educational Research Council
Social Science Program

The Human Adventure

Ancient Civilization

Prepared by the Social Science Staff of the Educational
Research Council of America

ALLYN AND BACON, INC.

Boston   Rockleigh, N.J.   Atlanta   Dallas   Belmont, Calif.

THE HUMAN ADVENTURE SERIES WAS PREPARED BY THE FOLLOWING MEMBERS OF THE SOCIAL SCIENCE STAFF OF THE EDUCATIONAL RESEARCH COUNCIL OF AMERICA:

NANCY BOSTICK, CONSTANCE BURTON, NANCY HENDERSON, MICHAEL JOYCE, MARILYN McLAUGHLIN, AGNES MICHNAY, JAMES PACKARD, MARIE RICHARDS, MARY RITLEY, JUDITH WENTZ, MARLENE ZWEIG.

MARY CATHERINE McCARTHY, EDITOR-IN-CHIEF

RAYMOND ENGLISH, DIRECTOR

The Educational Research Council of America acknowledges the contributions of the Kettering Family Fund and the Martha Holden Jennings Foundation, which have made possible the Social Science Program of the Educational Research Council of America.

Cover by Barry Zaid, Push Pin Studios, Inc.

Title page photo by SCALA New York/Florence in the Baghdad Museum

CONTENTS

MAPS

ACKNOWLEDGMENTS

Preface — facing page 1, William Belknap, Rapho-Guillumette; p. 17, Jay Ward Productions, Inc.; **Chapter 1** — p. 18, painting by Victor Brauner from the collection of Mr. and Mrs. Jacques Gelman; p. 26, Trustees of the British Museum; p. 28, Trustees of the British Museum; p. 33, American Museum of Natural History; **Chapter 2** — p. 34, Georg Gerster, Rapho Guillumette; p. 36-37, Georg Gerster, Rapho Guillumette; p. 38, (left and top right) Baghdad Museum, SCALA New York/Florence, (bottom right) Trustees of the British Museum; p. 39, (top left) Trustees of the British Museum, (top right) Baghdad Museum, SCALA New York/Florence, (bottom) Carl E. Östman, Inc.; p. 41, Carl E. Östman, Inc.; p. 43, Historical Pictures Service, Chicago; p. 44, Editions Arthaud; p. 47, Courtesy George G. Cameron, The University of Michigan and the American Schools of Oriental Research; p. 50, Eliot Elisofon, The Jewish Museum; p. 52, (left) Baghdad Museum, SCALA New York/Florence, (right) The University Museum, Philadelphia; p. 53, Lee Boltin; p. 54, Baghdad Museum, SCALA New York/Florence; p. 56, Trustees of the British Museum; p. 57, Trustees of the British Museum; **Chapter 3** — p. 58, Art Reference Bureau; p. 61, Service de Documentation Photographique de la Réunion des Musées Nationaux; p. 62, Art Reference Bureau; p. 63, Art Reference Bureau; p. 64, Baghdad Museum, SCALA New York/Florence; p. 65, (left) The Republic of Iraq, Ministry of Culture and Information, (right) Damascus Museum, Syria (Marwan Musselmany); p. 67, Trustees of the British Museum; p. 68, (left) Lion Demon — Magnesite or crystalline limestone. About 3000 B. C. Guennol Collection of Mr. and Mrs. A. B. Martin, on loan at the Brooklyn Museum, New York. Height 8.4 cm., (top right) The Metropolitan Museum of Art, Rogers Fund, Purchase 1954, (bottom right) Baghdad Museum, SCALA New York/Florence; p. 69, (top left and right) Trustees of the British Museum, (bottom) The University Museum, Philadelphia; p. 71, The University Museum, Philadelphia; **Chapter 4** — p. 74, Oriental Institute, University of Chicago; p. 76, The University Museum, Philadelphia; p. 77, The University Museum, Philadelphia; p. 82, S. Giedon, *The Beginnings of Art* (vol. I of the *Eternal Present*), The A. W. Mellon Lectures in the Fine Arts, 1957. Copyright 1964 by the Trustees of the National Gallery of Art, Washington, D. C. Reproduced by Permission of Princeton University Press; p. 84 and 86 (top), adapted from S. N. Kramer, *The Sumerians*, with permission of the University of Chicago Press, p. 86, (bottom left) The Metropolitan Museum of Art, from the collection of the General Theological Seminary, (bottom right) Editions Arthaud; p. 87, Trustees of the British Museum; p. 88, The Republic of Iraq, Ministry of Culture and Information; p. 89, (top) Baghdad Museum, SCALA New York/Florence; p. 89, (middle and bottom) Trustees of the British Museum; p. 90, Editorial Photocolor Archives, Inc.; **Chapter 5** — p. 94, Tor Eigeland, Black Star; p. 95, The University Museum, Philadelphia; p. 96, Trustees of the British Museum; p. 98, Photographie Bulloz; p. 99, Baghdad Museum, SCALA New York/Florence; p. 100, (top) The University Museum, Philadelphia, (bottom) Oriental Institute, University of Chicago; p. 101, The Metropolitan Museum of Art, Purchase 1886; p. 102, Oriental Institute, University of Chicago; p. 103, Trustees of the British Museum; **Chapter 6** — p. 104, (top left) The Republic of Iraq, Ministry of Culture and Information, (middle right) Editorial Photocolor Archives, Inc., (bottom) Tor Eigeland, Black Star; p. 108, Art Reference Bureau; p. 109, Trustees of the British Museum; p. 111, Giraudon; p. 114, Baghdad Museum, SCALA New York/Florence; p. 117, Giraudon; **Chapter 7** — p. 118, (top) Trustees of the British Museum, (bottom) Karachi Museum, SCALA New York/Florence; p. 121, Gunther Reitz, PIX, Inc.; p. 123, Trustees of the British Museum; p. 124, (top) Editorial Photocolor Archives, Inc., (bottom) The Metropolitan Museum of Art, Museum Excavations, 1919-1920; Rogers Fund, supplemented by contribution of Edward S. Harkness; p. 125, (top left) Oriental Institute, University of Chicago, (top right) Editorial Photocolor Archives, Inc., (bottom) The Metropolitan Museum of Art, The Carnarvon Collection, Gift of Edward S. Harkness, 1926; p. 126, The Metropolitan Museum of Art, Fletcher Fund, 1919-1920, and Huntley Bequest, 1958; p. 128, Karachi Museum, SCALA New York/Florence; p. 129, Karachi Museum, SCALA New York/Florence; p. 130, (top) National Museum, New Delhi, (bottom) Harrison Forman; p. 131, (left) Harrison Forman, (top right and bottom right) Karachi Museum, SCALA, New York/Florence; p. 132, National Museum, New Delhi; p. 139, Trustees of the British Museum; p. 140, The Bettmann Archive; p. 141, Alan Band Associates; **Conclusion** — p. 142, (left) Oriental Institute, University of Chicago, (right) Tor Eigeland, Black Star

Illustrations and Charts: Amperzand Design, Inc., pp. 28, 60, 73, 83, 94; Lewis Cary, p. 66; Contis Studios, Inc., pp. 5, 6, 8, 9, 11, 12, 13, 15, 145; Educational Research Council of Greater Cleveland, pp. 107, 122; Nicholas Fasciano, p. 78; Bill Greer, p. 147; Victor A. Lazzaro, pp. 46, 47, 81; Arielle Mather, pp. 24, 31; Jerry Pinkney, p. 3.

Map design and compilation by Allyn and Bacon.

A NOTE TO STUDENTS

To help you find out things for yourself and to use the things you know, think about the problems and questions as you read. They are marked ►, ●, or ★.

These symbols mean:

- ►   easy to solve
- ●   harder to solve—more thinking is needed
- ★   something extra—usually requires research

Many words in this book are respelled to help you pronounce them. The key below will help you read the respellings.

a	hat, cap	j	jam, enjoy	u	cup, butter
ā	age, face	k	kind, seek	u̇	full, put
ã	care, air	l	land, coal	ü	rule, move
ä	father, far	m	me, am	ū	use, music
		n	no, in		
b	bad, rob	ng	long, bring	v	very, save
ch	child, much			w	will, woman
d	did, red	o	hot, rock	y	young, yet
		ō	open, go	z	zero, breeze
e	let, best	ô	order, all	zh	measure, seizure
ē	equal, be	oi	oil, voice		
ėr	term, learn	ou	house, out	ə	represents:
					a in about
f	fat, if	p	paper, cup		e in taken
g	go, bag	r	run, try		i in April
h	he, how	s	say, yes		o in lemon
		sh	she, rush		u in circus
i	it, pin	t	tell, it		
ī	ice, five	th	thin, both		
		ŧħ	then, smooth		

From THORNDIKE-BARNHART JUNIOR DICTIONARY by E. L. Thorndike and Clarence L. Barnhart. Copyright © 1968 by Scott, Foresman and Company.

Locating Ourselves in Time and Space

We are about to begin an adventure. It is a human adventure—an adventure of man. The adventure will take us through thousands of years across thousands of miles. At every point in the adventure, we will need to know where we are in *time*. Are we talking about time 100 years ago, or 1,000 years ago, or 6,000 years ago? We will also need to know where we are in *space*. Are we in India, or China, or the United States, or where?

To locate ourselves in time, we need to learn how time is measured. Time is measured by the movement of the earth. The earth is our biggest clock! To locate ourselves in space, we need to learn about places on the earth. We will do this by studying maps and the globe.

First, let us visit a world where time seems a bit strange.

A Topsy-Turvy World

Do you know the story of Alice Through the Looking Glass? In the story, Alice goes through a looking glass, or mirror, into a topsy-turvy world. Alice was like the rest of us. She was used to a world of order. She found the other world very strange indeed. She was mixed up. Even telling time was not what Alice was used to.

Let us read one of Alice's adventures. Here she is talking with the White Queen. The Queen wants Alice to be her maid. She offers to pay Alice two pennies a week and give her jam every *other* day.

AN ADVENTURE THROUGH THE LOOKING GLASS

Alice couldn't help laughing as she said, "I don't want you to hire me — and I don't care for jam."

"It's very good jam," said the Queen.

"Well, I don't want any *today*, at any rate."

"You couldn't have it if you *did* want it," the Queen said. "The rule is, jam tomorrow and jam yesterday — but never jam today."

"It *must* come sometimes to jam today," Alice objected.

"No, it can't," said the Queen. "It's jam every *other* day: today isn't any *other* day, you know."

"I don't understand you," said Alice. "It's dreadfully confusing!"

"That's the effect of living backwards," the Queen said kindly: "it always makes one a little giddy at first —"

"Living backwards!" Alice repeated in great astonishment. "I never heard of such a thing!"

"— but there's one great advantage in it, that one's memory works both ways."

"I'm sure *mine* only works one way," Alice remarked. "I can't remember things before they happen."

"It's a poor sort of memory that only works backwards," the Queen remarked.

"What sort of things do *you* remember best?" Alice ventured to ask.

"Oh, things that happen the week after next," the Queen replied in a careless tone. "For instance, now," she went on, sticking a large piece of plaster on her finger as she spoke, "there's the King's Messenger. He's in prison now, being punished: and the trial doesn't even begin till next Wednesday: and of course the crime comes last of all."

"Suppose he never commits the crime?" said Alice.

"That would be all the better, wouldn't it?" The Queen said, as she bound the plaster round her finger with a bit of ribbon.

Alice felt there was no denying *that*. "Of course it would be all the better," she said: "but it wouldn't be all the better his being punished."

"You're wrong *there*, at any rate," said the Queen. "Were *you* ever punished?"

"Only for faults," said Alice.

"And you were all the better for it, I know!" the Queen said triumphantly.

"Yes, but then I *had* done the things I was punished for," said Alice: "that makes all the difference."

"But if you *hadn't* done them," the Queen said, "that would have been better still; better, and better, and better!" Her voice went higher with each "better," till it got quite to a squeak at last.

Alice was just beginning to say "There's a mistake somewhere—" when the Queen began screaming so loud that she had to leave the sentence unfinished. "Oh, oh, oh!" shouted the Queen, shaking her hand about as if she wanted to shake it off. "My finger's bleeding! Oh, oh, oh, oh!"

Her screams were so exactly like the whistle of a steam engine, that Alice had to hold both her hands over her ears.

"What *is* the matter?" she said, as soon as there was a chance of making herself heard. "Have you pricked your finger?"

"I haven't pricked it *yet*," the Queen said, "but I soon shall—oh, oh, oh!"

"When do you expect to do it?" Alice asked, feeling very much inclined to laugh.

"When I fasten my shawl again," the poor Queen groaned out: "the brooch will come undone directly. Oh, oh!" As she said the words the brooch flew open, and the Queen clutched wildly at it, and tried to clasp it again.

"Take care!" cried Alice. "You're holding it all crooked!" And she caught at the brooch; but it was too late: the pin had slipped, and the Queen had pricked her finger.

"That accounts for the bleeding, you see," she said to Alice with a smile. "Now you understand the way things happen here."

"But why don't you scream *now*?" Alice asked, holding her hands ready to put over her ears again.

"Why, I've done all the screaming already," said the Queen. "What would be the good of having it all over again?"

- Why was Alice mixed up? Explain her problem in your own words. Have you ever been mixed up in the same way? When? What happened?

- How do things look when you see them in a mirror or a looking glass? After Alice went through the looking glass, what did she learn about time in the topsy-turvy world?

In the looking-glass world, Alice could not locate herself. We are going to learn how to locate ourselves. We are going to learn about our world of order. How can we locate ourselves in time?

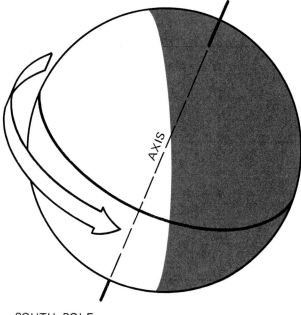

NORTH POLE

AXIS

SOUTH POLE

Using the Earth as a Clock: Rotation and Revolution

On most clocks the hands go around. One hand tells seconds. One tells minutes. One tells the hours. The earth we live on goes around, too. As it goes around, it tells, or causes, days and years. Let us review the movements of the earth.

The earth goes around on its **axis**. We say the earth **rotates** on its axis. We call one complete **rotation** a *day*. The earth also goes around the sun. We say it **revolves** around the sun. One complete **revolution** takes $365\frac{1}{4}$ days. We call this a *year*.

► Look at the diagram above. What movement of the earth does it show?

► Look at the diagram on page 6. What two movements of the earth does it show?

► What movement does the earth complete every day? How do we divide up a day?

► What movement does the earth complete every $365\frac{1}{4}$ days?

- What causes night and day?

★ How does the earth's revolution give us *seasons* of the year?

★ What is a *leap year*? Why do we have leap years?

Because of rotation and revolution, we can use the earth to measure time. We can use the earth as a clock of history. The earth goes on and on. It marks off the days. It marks off the years. It has marked off millions and millions of years.

Let us say that the earth has rotated on its axis seven times. Seven rotations make seven days. We call that much time a *week*. Now think about the earth as it revolves.

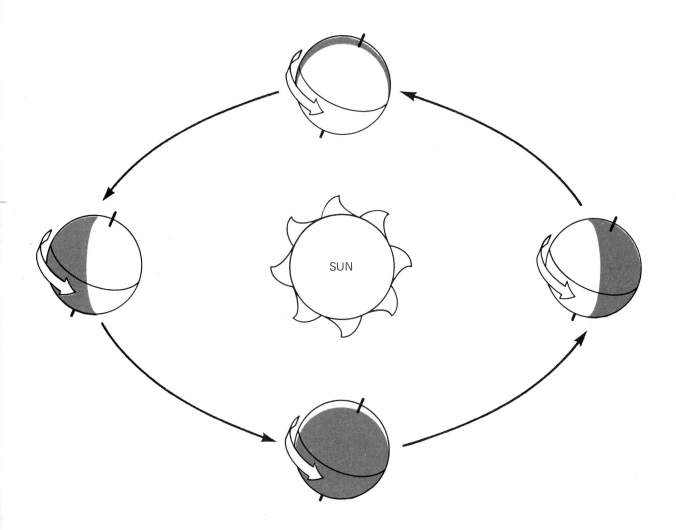

Suppose the earth has revolved around the sun ten times. Ten revolutions equal ten years. We call that much time a **decade.** Now suppose the earth has revolved around the sun 100 times. That equals 100 years, and we call that much time a **century.** Let us say that the earth has revolved around the sun 1,000 times. That equals 1,000 years. We call that much time a **millennium.**

▶ How many years are there in four decades? *40 yrs*

▶ How many years are there in seven and one-half centuries? *750 yrs.*

● The plural of millennium is *millennia.* How many years are there in six millennia? *6000 yrs*

● Do you tell your age in years or decades? Which of the new words would you use to tell about how long ago cave men lived? Which of the new words would you use to tell about how long ago Columbus landed in America? Which of the new words would you use to tell about how long ago the airplane was invented? *dec. mill. cent decades*

● Explain why we need different words for different lengths of time.

How We Number the Years

Now we know some words to use when we want to measure time. But we need a starting point! When we want to use a map, we must know where we are starting.

It is the same with time. When we want to measure time we must know where we are starting. You might say, "What's the problem? We're starting from today!" You would be right. We know what the date is today. But how did we get that date? When did men start counting to make today the date it is, and not some other date?

In the past, men have used many different *calendars.* Each of these calendars had a different starting point in time. Today, however, most men use the same calendar. This calendar measures time from the year when Jesus Christ was born. That year is called A.D. 1. **A.D.** is short for **anno Domini** (an'ō dom'ə nī). These are Latin words. They mean "In the Year of Our Lord." So A.D. 1 means In the Year of Our Lord, number one.

▶ We are living in A.D. 19??. What does that date mean?

★ Some people use the letters C.E. instead of A.D. What does C.E. stand for?

What about the years before A.D. 1? Many human beings lived during those years. We date those years by numbering them *backwards*, beginning from A.D. 1. Thus, the year before A.D. 1 is 1 B.C. (We write A.D. *before* a number and B.C. *after* a number.) B.C. means **before Christ**. Look at the time line below to see how this works.

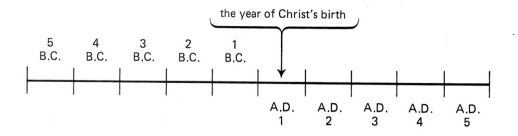

● Compare this line with a number line for mathematics showing *positive* and *negative integers*. What difference can you see?

How We Number the Centuries

Let us look at a time line that shows longer periods of time. Here is one. It shows *centuries*.

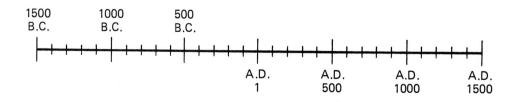

▶ Show where 800 B.C. is. Then show where these dates are:

A.D. 400	A.D. 975
A.D. 1250	A.D. 250
1125 B.C.	300 B.C.

How old are you? If you are ten, you are in your *eleventh* year of life! If you are nine, you are in your *tenth* year of life! If you are eleven, you are in your *twelfth* year of life! Why? Think of a newborn baby. He is in his *first* year of life. The very day after his first birthday, he begins the *second* year of his life. Still, we say that he is *one* year old. It is almost as if he were a year ahead of himself! We number centuries in the same way. Look at the time lines below to see how this system works.

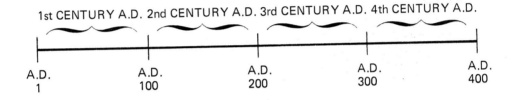

All the years from A.D. 1 *through* A.D. 100 are part of the first century A.D. All the years from A.D. 101 *through* A.D. 200 are part of the second century A.D. All the years from A.D. 1901 *through* the year A.D. 2000 are in the twentieth century A.D.

▶ What years make up the fourteenth century A.D.? The ninth century A.D.? The sixth century A.D.?

The same system is used for naming the centuries that came before Christ.

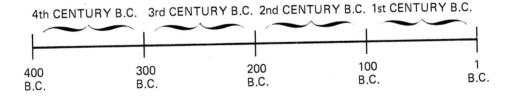

All the years from 1 B.C. *through* 100 B.C. are in the first century B.C. All the years from 101 B.C. *through* 200 B.C. are in the second century B.C.

▶ What years make up the eighth century B.C.? The thirteenth century B.C.? The fifth century B.C.?

Locating Ourselves in Time

Now we can locate ourselves in time. We know where we start in measuring time, and we know where we are right now in time. We know how things that happened can be put into their right order in time. We are almost ready to begin our adventure. Before we do, let us try out some of the things we have learned.

questions

▶   In what century are the following years?

    A.D. 1492   A.D. 1066

    331 B.C.   1350 B.C.

    A.D. 1776   A.D. 1861

▶   We name millennia in the same way that we name centuries. In what millennium is each of the following?

    A.D. 1970   2500 B.C.

    903 B.C.   A.D. 807

Locating Ourselves in Space: Grid Lines

In order to begin our adventure, we must be sure of one more thing. We must be sure we can locate ourselves in space, on the earth's curved surface. We already know a lot about how to locate ourselves on a *flat* surface. Let us review some of what we know.

Road maps have lines on them that help us to locate places on the map. The lines most often run north-south and east-west. The crisscrossing of these lines makes a **grid**. The lines are called **grid lines**. Maps with grid lines on them are called **grid maps**.

The grid lines divide the grid map into sections or squares. They make the map look like a large checkerboard. The spaces between the lines are numbered or lettered. The numbers help us to find cities according to their *east-west location*. The letters help us to find cities according to their *north-south location*. Together, they give us **reference points**, a way of describing the location of a place on a grid.

▶   On the grid map that follows, what is the location of Central City? Of North Rapids? Of East Central City?

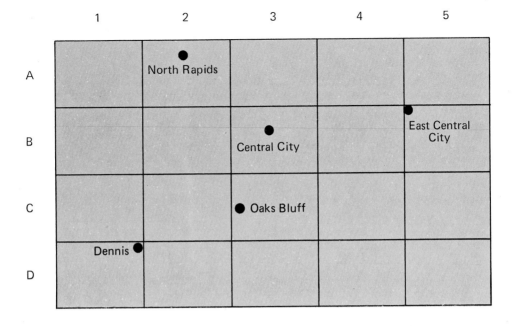

Locating Places on the Globe: Latitude and Longitude

The grid system works very well for a flat surface. But the surface of the globe, and the surface of our earth, are not flat. They are curved. In fact, the earth is like a huge ball. Because it is round, it has no beginning or end. A grid system is difficult to make on a curved surface. But we need such a system.

● Put a dot on a ball. Now try to describe the location of the dot on the ball. Why is that so hard to do?

Luckily, our earth is not a ball which can roll in just any direction. It rotates on its axis. This rotation gives us two fixed reference points—the ends of the axis. We call these ends of the axis the poles. The north and south poles are the only points on the earth's surface that remain fixed while the earth rotates. As you know, these points are not marked on the earth.

We need another reference point for our system, however. First, we find a point on the earth's surface halfway between the poles. Then we use this point to draw a circle around the earth. We call this circle the **equator**. Equator comes from *equal*. The equator is an equal distance from the poles.

► Look at the globe. Hold it so that you are looking straight down on the north pole. The north pole is now in the center. How far south can you see?

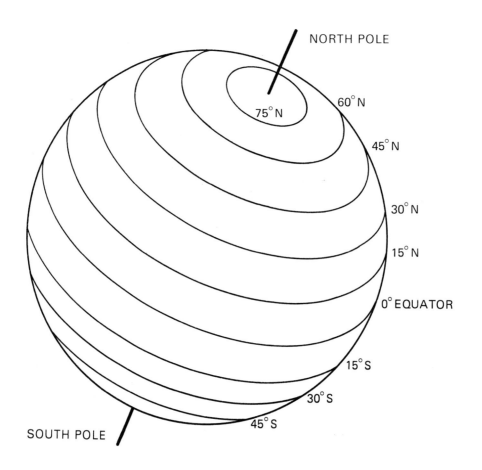

When you hold the globe and look straight down on the north pole, you can see most of the northern **hemisphere**. But you cannot see the equator at the outer rim of the globe. As you look *from the equator* toward the north pole, you will see circles that get smaller as they get closer to the pole. As you look *toward the equator* from the north pole, you will see that the circles get larger as they get closer to the equator. We call these circles **parallels of latitude**.

All points along a parallel are the same distance from the equator. The parallels tell how far north or south any given point is from the equator. We use the parallels as **reference lines**. Each parallel has its own number, from zero (the equator) to 90 (each pole). Its number tells how far north or south it is from the equator.

- Now look at your globe again. Find a second set of lines on it that cross the parallels. Do these lines run east and west, as the parallels do? If not, in what direction do they run?

This set of lines divides the globe into sections like an orange. The lines are called **meridians**. If we label one of these meridians zero, we can use the meridians to tell how far east or west we are. We can tell by counting how many meridians east or west of the "zero" meridian we are. The meridians are called the **lines of longitude.**

We saw that the parallels are numbered from zero to 90 north and from zero to 90 south. The distances north or south from the equator are called degrees. These are called **degrees of latitude**. The distances east or west from the zero meridian are also called degrees. These are called **degrees of longitude**. The lines of longitude run from pole to pole. Zero meridian is also called the **prime meridian**. There are 180 degrees (180°) of longitude west of the prime meridian. There are also 180 degrees (180°) of longitude east of the prime meridian.

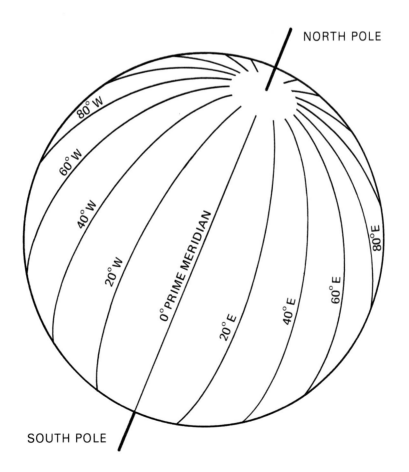

Our grid system for a round surface works like this. If you draw a line north or south on the globe, you cross the *parallels—* or *lines of latitude.* If you draw a line east or west on the globe, you cross the *meridians—* or *lines of longitude.* Thus we have a pattern of latitude and longitude lines. This pattern is a grid system that works for a round surface. The system helps us to locate any spot on earth. We can take the system from a round surface and use it on a flat surface like this page!

Here is a help to remembering which lines are latitude and which are longitude. Latitude comes from a word meaning *broad.* Longitude comes from *long.* Look at a map and tell why the "long" in longitude helps you to remember which lines are longitude?

▶ Look at the picture of the globe on page 12. What do we call the lines on this globe? (Clue: The lines run from east to west.)

● If we follow one of these lines on a globe, what geometrical shape will we draw?

▶ Look at the picture of the globe on page 13. What do we call the lines on this globe? (Clue: The lines run from north to south.)

● If we follow one of these lines on a globe, what geometrical shape will we draw?

▶ Look at the picture of the globe on page 15. Point out the meridians of longitude. Point out the parallels of latitude.

▶ On a globe in your classroom find the *prime meridian.*

▶ Look at the globe again. Put your finger on latitude 35°N and longitude 40°E. This is part of the land that is called the Middle East. Now find the same place on the map on page 16.
  What is the latitude of place X?
  What is the longitude of place Y?
  Give the latitude and the longitude of place Z.

● The city of Baghdad is closest to one of these four locations. Which one?
  (a) 35°N, 45°E   (c) 45°N, 35°E
  (b) 35°N, 44°E   (d) 45°N, 33°E

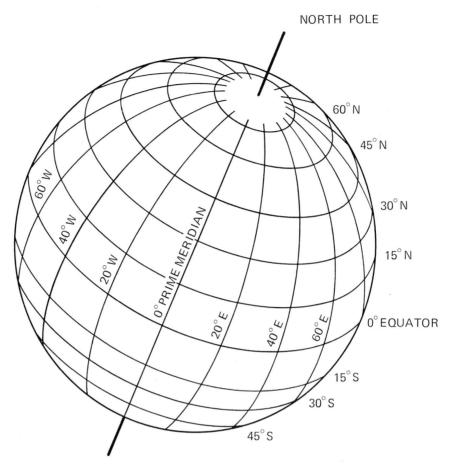

NORTH POLE

60° N
45° N
30° N
15° N
0° EQUATOR
15° S
30° S
45° S

60° W
40° W
20° W
0° PRIME MERIDIAN
20° E
40° E
60° E

SOUTH POLE

● Look at a globe again. What major city of the world is located near 30°N, 30°E? Now locate that city on the map on page 16.

● Look at an atlas. Which one of these four cities in the United States is located at about the same latitude as Baghdad?

New York   New Orleans
Chicago   Los Angeles

★ What does *parallel* mean? Why are the lines of latitude called parallels?

★ The word *meridian* comes from a Latin word meaning *midday*. Find out why we use the word for the lines that measure degrees east and west of the prime meridian. How do the meridians divide the earth into *time zones*? What do they have to do with the rotation of the earth? How does knowing the longitude of a place help you to know the time of day or night in that place?

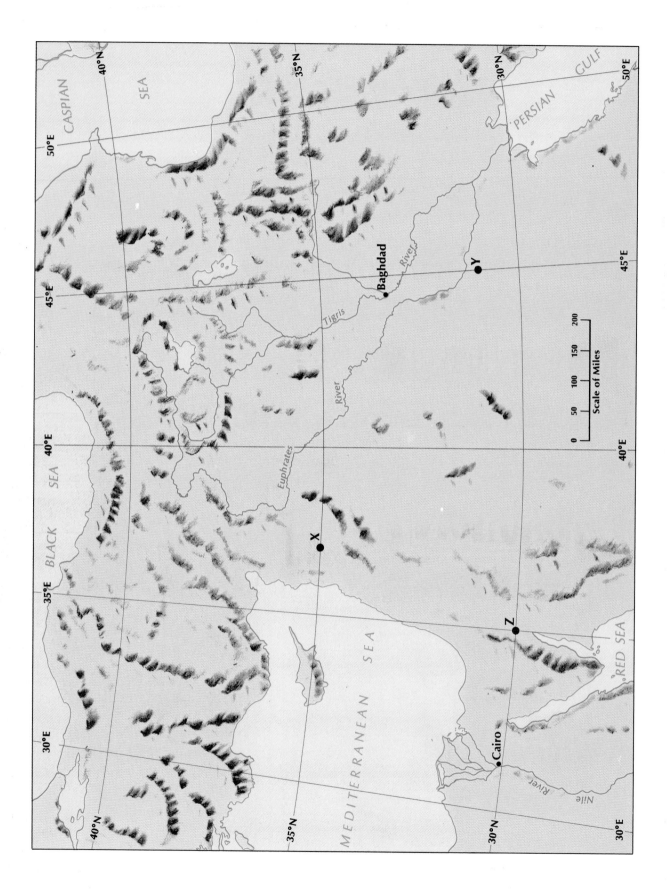

Here We Go in Time and Space!

Now we know how to locate ourselves in both time and space. We are ready to begin *The Human Adventure*. We will always be sure just *where* we are, and just *when* we are there. Back, back, back we go—through years, centuries, millennia! Far, far, far away we go—to another part of the earth!

This painting, "Prelude to a Civilization," is a twentieth-century artist's representation of early man.

chapter 1

Man's Great Leap Forward

It is hard for us to imagine what kind of life early man lived. His life was often filled with danger and hard work. His choices were limited by the kind of land and climate he lived in. His choices were also limited by the plants and animals he found around him. These four things—land and climate, plants and animals—are called **natural**, or **physical**, **environment**. Early man was limited by his physical environment.

Early man slowly learned how to work with his physical environment. He even learned how to change some of it. He still had to depend on his environment, but he was beginning to *control* it. He learned skills that allowed him to do so. These skills made the big difference in his life.

Let us see how early man slowly took control of his physical environment. Then we shall see what was his great leap forward. We will also learn how he was able to make that leap.

Man the Food-Gatherer and Hunter

Early man got his food about the same way that wild animals do today. He found nuts and berries and fruits to eat. He hunted and killed animals. He fished. He spent most of his time finding enough food to keep alive. When he could not find enough food, he sometimes starved to death.

To stay alive, early man had to go where the food was. First he would eat all the nuts, berries, and fruits in one place. Then he would move on to another place to find more. He followed the animal herds to get meat and skins. He had to be a wanderer. His physical environment left him no other choice.

Yet, early man was not just another animal. He could *think*. This was the main difference between him and the animals. He used his brains to think of new ways of doing things. He watched animals and saw how well they could do some things. He saw what food they ate. He learned from them.

There was another difference between early man and the animals. He stood on two feet instead of four. That left his hands free. With free hands, he could do some of the things he had thought of doing. Early man made weapons of stone, and later of bone. He made traps to catch small animals. He made nets to catch fish and birds. He used animal skins to make clothes. He used fire to hunt, to keep warm, and to keep himself safe.

Most important of all, early man was able to *remember* what he saw and did. He taught his children what he learned. Because he did all these things, early man was a thinker, a learner, and a teacher.

- What are some things that early man could have learned from animals?

- Think of some ways in which animals teach their young.

- In what ways might early man have taught his children?

- What were important differences between the ways in which early man and animals taught their young?

- What are some ways in which man teaches his children today? What are some ways in which he teaches other men?

The Move to Mesopotamia

By 10,000 B.C., the last of the huge icecaps of the Ice Age had melted. The climate changed. Heavy forests grew up in northern Eurasia, where the ice had been. The grasslands that were south of the Mediterranean Sea turned into deserts. That is how great deserts like the Sahara and the Arabian Deserts were formed.

Between these two regions—the forest region in northern Eurasia and the desert region south of the Mediterranean Sea— lay another region. This region was located *east* of the Mediterranean Sea. It was called Mesopotamia (mes'ə pə tā'mē ə).

Mesopotamia means "the land between two rivers." The land was given that name because it lay between two rivers, the

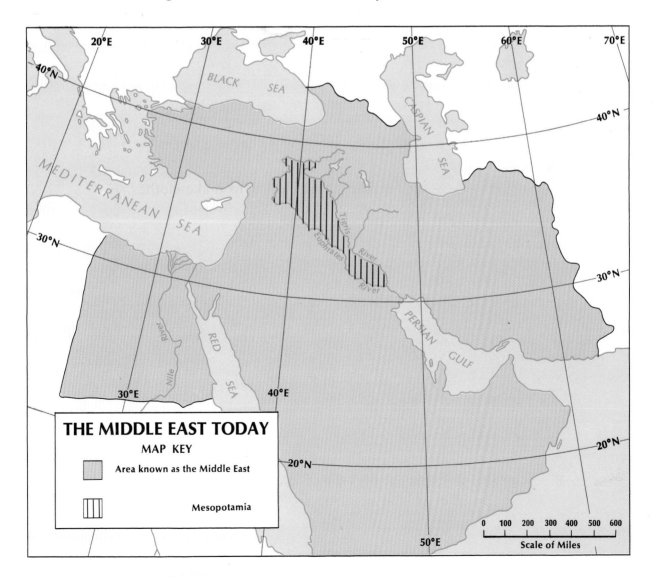

THE MIDDLE EAST TODAY

MAP KEY

Area known as the Middle East

Mesopotamia

Tigris (tī′ gris) and the Euphrates (ū frā′ tēz). Mesopotamia was part of the land that today we call the Middle East. Locate Mesopotamia and the two rivers on the map on page 21. Then find the same area on a globe in your classroom.

▶ Look at the map on page 23. In what areas are the mountains? The plateaus? The plains?

▶ What are the sources of the two rivers that flow through Mesopotamia? Into what body of water do they flow?

▶ Describe the physical features of northern Mesopotamia. Describe the physical features of southern Mesopotamia.

Northern Mesopotamia was the life-giving part of the Middle East. The land and climate gave men many choices. The summers were long, hot, and dry, just as they are today. The winters were mild and rainy, just as they are today. The melting snow on the mountain tops kept rivers and streams flowing throughout the year. Grasses grew in the spring. They dried up under the hot summer sun. In the winter, however, rains brought them back to life. Trees grew among the grasses and along the riverbanks. The sides of the hills and low mountains were covered with trees.

People left the desert region south of the Mediterranean Sea. They looked for better lands. Some of these people moved north and west, into the forest region. Others moved into northern Mesopotamia. Many scholars believe that man made a great leap forward in Mesopotamia. They think it was there that he learned, little by little, to control his physical environment.

Man the Producer of Food

Great change did not take place all at once, however. Man was not a hunter and gatherer one day and a farmer the next. The change took place very slowly.

The first producers of food were probably women. In the centuries just before 6500 B.C., women learned to cut wheat and barley grasses. These grains grew wild along the hillsides. Next, the women made an important discovery. They learned to let some of the ripe grain seeds drop to the ground and stay there.

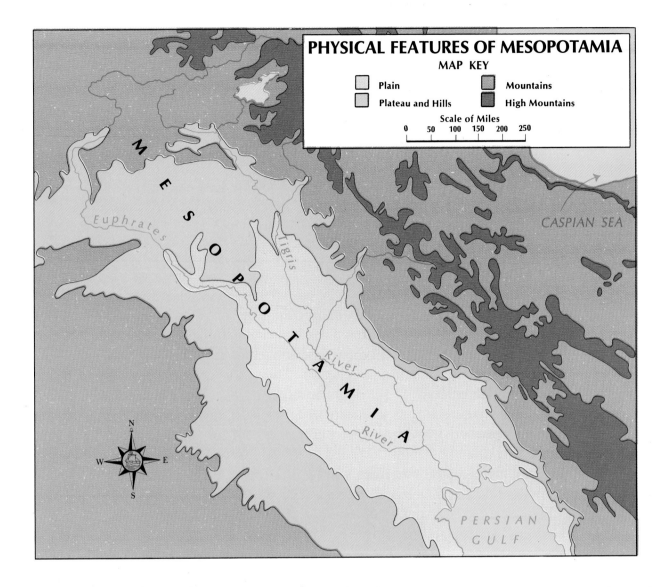

PHYSICAL FEATURES OF MESOPOTAMIA

MAP KEY

Plain

Plateau and Hills

Mountains

High Mountains

Scale of Miles

0   50   100   150   200   250

If they did, then even more grasses would grow in that place the next year. Finally, the women learned that they could make grasses grow in fields where such grasses did not usually grow.

▶ Can you guess how the women learned to grow things on purpose?

The women broke the ground with sharp-pointed digging sticks. Then they planted seeds *on purpose*. Planting seeds on purpose was the beginning of agriculture. The women who planted the seeds were the first farmers. Agriculture was a very important change indeed. It meant that man was beginning to control his physical environment.

● Why do you think that women were probably the first growers of food?

● Why did the beginning of agriculture mean that man was beginning to control his physical environment?

● The kind of agriculture described here is called *seed agriculture*. A different kind of agriculture started in another part of the Old World. It is called *root agriculture*. From its name, how do you think root agriculture is different from seed agriculture?

In hilly country between rivers, trees shaded the ground. Few grasses would grow in the shade. That meant the farmers would not have to cut through many tough grass roots. The soil would be fairly loose and easy to dig.

These early farmers had seen animals eating the bark of trees. The trees died soon afterwards. The early farmers learned from what they saw. They chose a small area and slashed the bark of all the trees that were growing there. They also dug the ground between the trees and planted seeds for grains. They knew that soon the trees would die. Their leaves would fall off. The soil around the dead trees would get more sunlight. Then the grains would grow better than ever before!

Slash-and-burn agriculture

The farmers also learned that fire could be a great help. They often burned the bushes and grass under the dead trees. Then they scattered the ashes over the soil. This helped to keep the soil rich, or fertile.

● This way of farming is called *slash-and-burn agriculture.* Is that a good name for it? Why or why not?

Before three millennia had passed, the practice of agriculture was common in many parts of the Old World. By 3500 B.C., there were farmers in western Eurasia, the part of the world we now call Europe. There were farmers along the northern coast of Africa. There were farmers in India and China, too. Locate these farming areas on a classroom map of the world.

Man the Tamer of Animals

Because of the development of agriculture, the human population grew. Agriculture brought more food. Fewer people starved. The area around the grain fields was not good for wild animals, however. Many of them left. When they did, the hunters lost much of their food supply. As time passed, the hunters found fewer and fewer animals. This was very hard for the hunters. They had always needed great skill. Now they needed even more skill if they wanted to eat meat.

Some men chose to remain hunters anyway. They followed the animals into different regions. Agriculture was still mostly "women's work," but some men began to share in it. Certainly it was a safer and surer way to get food than hunting. Still other men began to catch some of the wild animals that had stayed behind. Instead of killing them, they tamed them and kept them in a herd. Keeping a small herd of goats or cattle meant that they could be sure of having meat close at hand.

The herders watched the tame goats and cattle feed their young with milk. They thought, "Why don't we milk the goats and cattle for our own food? Why don't we use the sheep's fuzzy skin for our clothing?" Over the centuries, thoughts like these led many men to become herders. Keeping herds was another way for man to gain more control over the physical environment.

Herders and Farmers

What was it like to live in northern Mesopotamia about 4000 B.C.? We don't know many details. We do know that some men and women were living in villages. They were mainly food producers. Probably they kept a few animals, too. Other men and women lived outside the villages. They kept herds. They did not stay in any one place long enough to farm. These herders kept moving back and forth to find food and water for their animals. In the summer they moved to the hills. In the winter they returned to the low grasslands.

● Remember what you read about the climate in northern Mesopotamia. Why did the herders have to move when the seasons changed?

Herding became more important in the grassland areas. There, the tough grass roots made digging hard for the farmers. In the other areas, the soil could be dug up easily. There, farming became more important. In northern Mesopotamia, herding and farming had become the two important ways of life. The men who got all their food by hunting had almost disappeared from the region. They had followed the game animals into other regions.

The herders and farmers discovered that they could help each other. The herders could supply meat to the farmers. In their travels, they could also find things that the farmers could use. One of these things was stone for tools. In return, the farmers could supply grain to the herders. They could also supply them with grain stalks that were left over from the grain. The stalks were good for the animal herds to feed on.

The herders and farmers were not always friendly. Sometimes there was trouble between them. The herders might feel that they were the only ones who had the right to use a certain area of land. The farmers might feel the same way. When that happened, there was often a fight to decide who would use the land.

- Read the Old Testament story about Cain and Abel. How did these two brothers earn their living?

- There were fights between herders and farmers in the American West. Tell what these fights were about.

More Discoveries

The early farmers had invented a simple spade and hoe. That made their work a little easier than it had been with a digging stick. After a time, farmers also invented a foot plow. This plow had a long curved handle. Just above the blade, it had a small peg. The farmer would put his foot on the peg. Then he would use his weight to push the blade into the ground. The foot plow was a better tool than the digging stick, the spade, or the hoe. Later, one man pulled the plow with a rope. Another man guided and pushed it.

Centuries after the plow was invented, someone got a bright idea. Men had to pull the plow. Why not hitch it to an animal instead? The idea was tried. Suddenly there was an easier way to plow the ground! Man had learned that by using his mind, he would not have to use his muscles so often. He could make animals use *their* muscles instead.

THE CLIMATE OF SOUTHERN MESOPOTAMIA

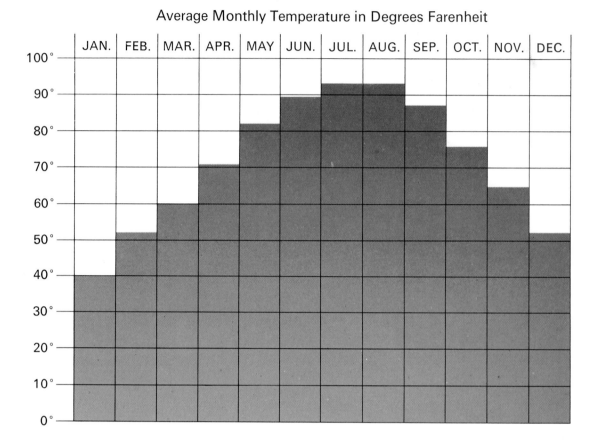

Average Monthly Temperature in Degrees Farenheit

| | JAN. | FEB. | MAR. | APR. | MAY | JUN. | JUL. | AUG. | SEP. | OCT. | NOV. | DEC. |

Average Monthly Precipitation in Inches

| | JAN. | FEB. | MAR. | APR. | MAY | JUN. | JUL. | AUG. | SEP. | OCT. | NOV. | DEC. |

These bar graphs show the average monthly temperatures and precipitation for Baghdad, a city in Mesopotamia today. What do the graphs tell you about the summers in southern Mesopotamia? What do they tell you about the rainfall?

The Move to Sumer

The population in Mesopotamia was growing. The more people there were, the less land there was for each farming family. After a few years, the soil seemed to be worn out. It would no longer grow good crops. Then the farmers had to clear land for new fields by using slash-and-burn agriculture.

To find new land, both farmers and herders began to move out of northern Mesopotamia. They went in every direction. The Tigris and Euphrates Rivers were the "roads" leading to the south. Many farmers followed these roads. They set up new villages in river valleys toward the south.

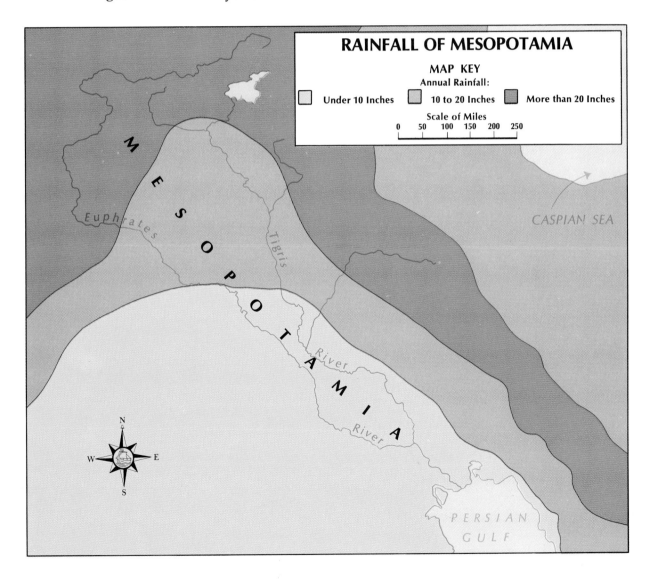

RAINFALL OF MESOPOTAMIA

MAP KEY
Annual Rainfall:

Under 10 Inches   10 to 20 Inches   More than 20 Inches

Scale of Miles
0   50   100   150   200   250

CASPIAN SEA

PERSIAN GULF

What was the new land like? The land between the rivers was a **flood plain**. Every year, in the spring, the rivers flooded. After the flood waters went down, the land was covered by a layer of rich soil. This soil was free of stones and tough roots. The low-lying land was swampy. Many kinds of waterfowl and fish could be caught. Date palm trees grew wild along the river banks.

The population in the river valleys kept growing. Growing population meant a growing need for land. Some people pushed on farther south, toward the mouth of the two rivers. There, in southern Mesopotamia, the climate was even hotter and drier.

▶ Look at the map on page 29. About how much rain falls in southern Mesopotamia in a year?

▶ How does this rainfall compare to the rainfall in northern Mesopotamia?

In ancient times, the land of southern Mesopotamia was known as **Sumer** (sü′ mər). To us, Sumer may not seem like a very good place for men to live. Yet Sumer was the land where, for the first time, man really took control of his physical environment. Let us see how he was able to take this control.

The people in Sumer wanted to grow crops. They also needed water. What good was rich soil if there was no rain? If seeds were planted in the spring, they would die during the hot, rainless season. To solve this problem, man, the thinker, went to work again. He watched for clues and he found one.

Every spring the rivers flooded. As the flood waters went down, they left **silt** along the river banks. Silt is made up of sand and soil carried along by the river waters. Year after year, this silt built up until it formed natural **levees** (lev′ ēz), or banks of soil. These levees gave men the clue they needed to solve their water problem.

What they did was to build up the levees. They brought more soil to make the levees higher and stronger. Then the levees would give them some protection from severe floods. They also learned to use the levees in another way. When the fields became too dry in the summer, men poked holes in the levees. The water would come pouring out. The men would dig little channels to carry the water to their crops.

Sumerians built up the levees and let water run out into the fields.

In time, the men of Sumer made these little channels bigger. Eventually the channels became canals. Many of the canals ran for miles and miles, bringing water from the levees to the crops. This way of watering the land is called **irrigation**. Because of irrigation, the Sumerians (sü mēr' ē ənz) did not have to depend entirely on rain to grow their crops. Man was taking more and more control over his physical environment.

Miles of canals carried water to the crops.

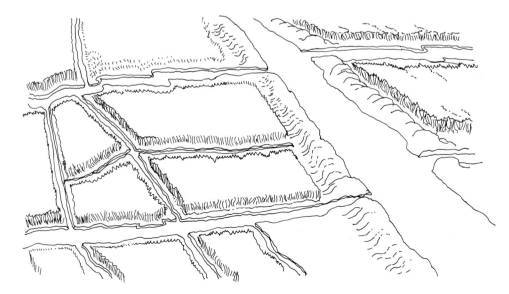

Man the Maker of Surplus

The farmers of Sumer had rich soil. Thanks to the floods, it would stay rich. This soil would produce good crops. Thanks to irrigation, these crops would grow even in dry weather. The men of Sumer had animals to pull their plows. All these things helped the Sumerians to have bigger harvests than men had ever had before. They helped them to do their work more easily than men had ever done it before.

As a result, the farmers grew more than they or their families needed to eat. That means they grew a **surplus**. Year in and year out, the Sumerians grew surplus crops. *This surplus of food was an important part of man's great leap forward.*

Man the Specialist

Because there was a surplus of food, some men and women were free to do other special jobs. They no longer had to grow crops or tend herds. They became **specialists**. Some repaired the levees. Some repaired the canals. Some became pottery makers. Some made dried bricks of mud and used them to build houses. Others became religious leaders. Still others took charge of groups of workers and showed them how to work together better. Man was beginning to divide up the work. Everyone did something important, but not everyone had to do the same thing. *The division of labor was another important part of man's great leap forward.*

Man the Builder of Cities

The people of Sumer also began to live closer together. They learned to work together on big jobs like farming, irrigating, or building houses. They learned to depend on one another.

All these big jobs were hard work. They required planning. Still, the planning and work were worthwhile. These jobs meant that thousands and thousands of people could settle down permanently. The people no longer had to move on to find rich soil. Men and women, their children and grandchildren, could all stay in the same area. Thus, it became possible for men to build the first cities. *Cities were another important part of man's great leap forward.*

A model of a Sumerian city

Civilization—The Great Leap Forward

We have been talking about the time around 3500 B.C. What things happened at that particular time that helped man to become civilized? Why do we say that at that time in history, men built the *first civilization*?

Do you remember the title of this chapter? Now we know what "the great leap" was. It was civilization! Man came a long, hard way before he could make that leap.

What do we mean by **civilization** and **civilized**? These are two words that we will see again and again in the pages of *The Human Adventure*. They are big words and can mean many things. In our reading, they will always mean the same thing. When we talk about *civilization*, we will be talking about many people living together in one area. Three things must be true about these people:

1. They must have a *surplus of food.*
2. They must have *division of labor.*
3. They must have built *cities.*

We will say that people are *civilized* only if all three of these things are true about them.

Who were the first civilized men? What was the first civilization? Now you know the answers to these questions. Scholars believe that the first civilized men were the Sumerians. They lived in Sumer, land of the first civilization. These were the men who made the great leap forward. These were the men who opened the door for the Human Adventure to begin.

chapter 2

Solving the Mystery of Sumer

Civilization began more than 5,000 years ago in southern Mesopotamia. Working together, the Sumerians created a new way of life. They built the first known civilization on earth.

The Sumerians did many, many things for the first time in history. Then they were forgotten! Only 100 years ago, no one even knew their name. No one knew that such people had ever lived. Even when Sumer was found, it was found by accident! The men who found it were looking for traces of *other* ancient civilizations. Men learned later that these other civilizations came after Sumer.

The Forgotten People

Today we know many things about the forgotten Sumerians. We know something about their cities and their ideas. We know how they looked and how they lived. We know what they ate and what they wore. We know the songs they sang and the language they spoke. How do we know so many things about them? To answer that question, we must learn how men discover the secrets of the past.

Finding out about the past is like solving a mystery. Historians and **archaeologists** (är′ kē ol′ ə jists) help us to know what happened in the past. Historians learn about the past by studying written records. Archaeologists learn about the past by studying the objects that ancient peoples have left behind. These objects are called **artifacts**. The archaeologists find these artifacts by digging them up.

Historians and archaeologists are like detectives. The story of the discovery of Sumer is like a detective story. It is the story of how historians and archaeologists put together many clues to solve a great mystery. The clues led them first to discover other ancient civilizations. Finally, the clues led them to Sumer. What kinds of clues were they? Before you read on, see if you can think of what these clues might have been. Use these questions to help you.

- Suppose our own civilization disappeared and was forgotten. What traces of it might remain 5,000 years from now? What might future historians and archaeologists learn about us from these traces?

- Suppose you wanted to find out about a people. They lived long ago and left no written records. What other clues might they have left behind? What kind of clues would be likely to last through the centuries?

- Who would leave more clues—hunters or people who live in cities?

- Would it be easy to learn about ancient people from the clues they left behind? Why or why not?

▶ Look up the word *archaeology*. What does it mean?

How good a detective can *you* be? The following pages show pictures of Mesopotamia and of artifacts which were found there. Your problem is to discover something about the people who made these artifacts. The pictures will give you clues to what the Sumerians were like and to how they lived.

Archaeologists do many kinds of work in trying to uncover the secrets of the past. This man is picking away dirt to clear the stones of an ancient Sumerian pavement.

Painted pottery bowls

Stone statues of a Sumerian man and woman

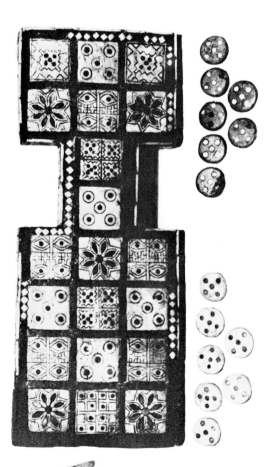

Gameboard and playing pieces

An example of Sumerian writing

Copper model of a donkey-drawn chariot

The point in Mesopotamia where the Tigris and Euphrates Rivers meet

The Sumerians left many clues behind them. Yet, the mystery of Sumer was not solved all at once. It was solved slowly, over many years. Let us read about how it was solved.

The First Clues: Old Stories

The first clues to the mystery of Sumer were written ones. They were old stories about ancient peoples. However, these clues did not lead straight back to the Sumerians. The stories described many other ancient peoples who lived in Mesopotamia long ago. These peoples lived there after the Sumerians. The Babylonians (bab′ ə lō′ nē ənz) were one of these ancient peoples.

The Babylonians were named for Babylon, their greatest city. The stories told about a time when the Babylonians were very powerful. At that time, there were wonderful palaces in Babylon. There were high walls and large temples. A mighty king of Babylon built some beautiful gardens on buildings that rose high into the air. These were known as the "Hanging Gardens of Babylon." Babylonian farmers grew large amounts of grain. Great Babylonian armies marched out of the city to conquer other lands.

▶ Find Babylon on the map on page 42. In what part of Mesopotamia was it located?

★ The Hanging Gardens were one of the Seven Wonders of the World. Find out what they looked like. Who built them and why?

Let us read two old stories about Babylon. The first one was written by Herodotus (hə rod′ ə təs). He was a great historian of the ancient world.

A STORY OF BABYLON

Very little rain falls in Babylon. There is just enough rain to make the grain begin to grow. After that, the plants must be irrigated with water from the Euphrates River. The waters of the Euphrates do not flood the grain fields naturally. Water must be spread across the land by hard work, canals, and buckets. The hard work produces wonderful results. Of all the countries that I have seen, no other produces so much grain.

Let me tell you how the Babylonians used to set up their marriages. Once a year, all the girls who were old enough to marry were brought together in one place. The men stood around them in a circle. Each girl in turn was offered up for sale as a wife. The pretty girls were sold first. Rich men who wanted wives bid against one another for the pretty girls. When all the pretty girls were gone, the plain girls were sold. The plainest girl would be asked to stand up. The poor men were asked who would take the least money to marry her. (The Babylonians thought that poor men had no use for pretty wives. They were paid to take the plain girls.) The poor men were paid with the money collected from the sale of the pretty girls. Marriages could be set up only in this way. It was against the law for a father to pick a husband for his daughter.

A reconstruction of the main gate of the walled city of Babylon

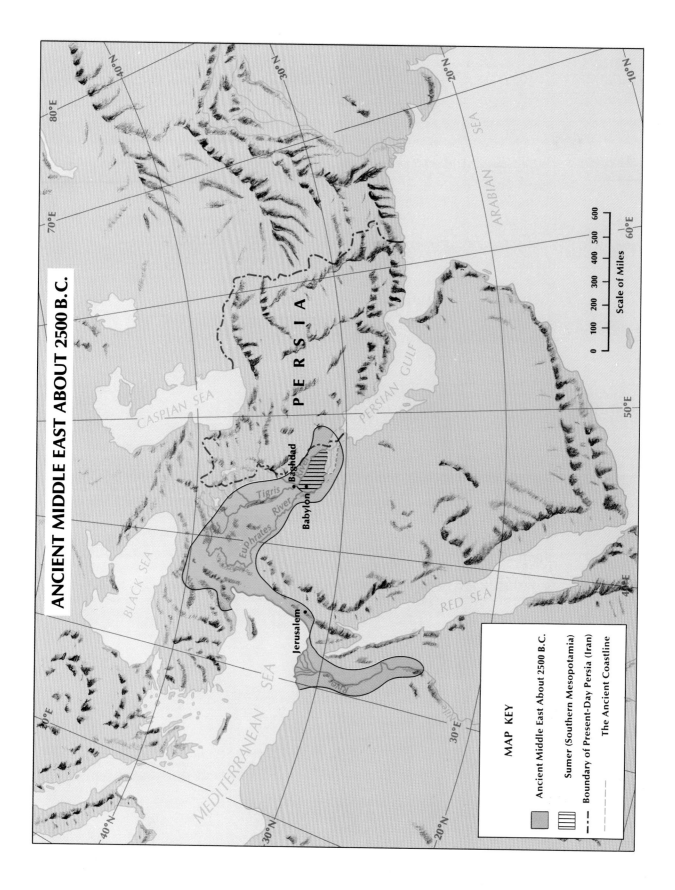

ANCIENT MIDDLE EAST ABOUT 2500 B.C.

CASPIAN SEA

BLACK SEA

MEDITERRANEAN SEA

RED SEA

ARABIAN SEA

PERSIAN GULF

P E R S I A

Tigris River

Euphrates River

Baghdad

Babylon

Jerusalem

Nile

Scale of Miles

0 100 200 300 400 500 600

MAP KEY

Ancient Middle East About 2500 B.C.

Sumer (Southern Mesopotamia)

Boundary of Present-Day Persia (Iran)

The Ancient Coastline

Other stories about the Babylonians are found in the Old Testament. That is where our second story comes from. This Bible story tells about armies that marched out of Babylon to conquer the city of Jerusalem.

► Find Jerusalem on the map on page 42. Is it in Mesopotamia? Where is it located?

THE STORY OF AN ATTACK ON JERUSALEM

In those days the king of Babylon was very powerful. His servants came up to Jerusalem and the city was attacked. And the king of Babylon came to the city while his servants were attacking it. And the king of Jerusalem gave himself up to the king of Babylon. He gave up himself and his mother, and his servants, and his princes, and his palace officials. The king of Babylon took him prisoner in the eighth year of his reign. And he also carried off all the treasures of the king's house and cut in pieces all the vessels of gold in the house of the Lord. He carried away captive all of Jerusalem. He carried away all the princes and all the brave warriors, 10,000 captives, and all the craftsmen. And none were left, except the poorest people of the land. Thus he carried away the king to Babylon and the king's mother, the king's wives, his officials, and the chief men of the land. And he took them all into captivity from Jerusalem to Babylon.

● What did you learn about the Babylonians from the two stories you just read? What did you learn about their way of life? How do you know that the Babylonians were rich and powerful?

An artist's view of Babylon

Through the centuries, many men remembered the stories of ancient peoples. Yet, they did not remember much about the peoples themselves. The stories described a part of the world that was very, very old. It had changed many times. Men lost track of just how many changes had taken place. The great cities disappeared. There were no longer rich fields of grain. Instead, the land was dry, dusty, and brown. It was a poor land. The old stories were all that was left of the greatness of Babylon and Mesopotamia.

● Why can the old stories be called "clues"? Why would it be difficult to prove that the stories were true?

The Second Clues: Mysterious Marks

About 350 years ago, an Italian scholar went to southern Mesopotamia. He looked for proof that the old stories were true. When he arrived, he saw that the land was very flat. Yet, here and there, he saw great **mounds**, or hills, that rose up to break the flatness. The people who lived in Mesopotamia called these mounds **tels**.

The Italian wondered what the *tels* could be. Near one of them, he found some square objects covered with strange marks. The objects were bricks. The marks on the bricks looked like the footprints of birds walking over wet sand.

When the Italian went home, he took some of the bricks with him. Scholars studied the strange marks on the bricks. They decided that the marks had been made by an ancient people. They said that the strange marks were a form of writing. They called this writing **cuneiform** (kū nē'ə fôrm) because each of the marks was shaped like a wedge. Cuneiform comes from a Latin word, *cuneus*, that means "wedge."

The bricks were an exciting discovery. They showed that people had once lived in southern Mesopotamia. No one understood what the marks meant. The scholars hoped that someday, someone would learn to read them. Then they could learn much more about the people who made the marks.

● How did the first clues lead to the second clues? How might the discovery of the bricks make people more interested in southern Mesopotamia?

● At first glance, would strange marks on little bricks seem to be very important? Why or why not?

★ Did the Italian who found the bricks use the methods of an historian or of an archaeologist? Explain.

The Third Clue: Tels and Tablets

Years passed. Men found more and more bricks with the strange writing on them. These clay tablets were found in different parts of Mesopotamia. Usually they were found near *tels*. After a time, men became more and more interested in the *tels*. They wondered what the *tels* were and how they got there. Today, we *know* the answers to these questions. Let us interrupt our story to learn what these *tels* are.

Archaeologists discovered that every *tel* is made up of the ruins of ancient cities. These cities were built one on top of another. These ancient cities were found all around southern Mesopotamia. But no one knew this because the cities had been covered up.

Tels are mounds of broken clay pottery, mud brick, dirt, and sand. There were few stones in these *tels*. Rock was scarce in southern Mesopotamia. To build their homes, the ancient people had to use materials they had at hand. These materials were river mud and river clay.

The ancient peoples built their homes on high ground. This protected them from floods. The houses were made mainly from clay and mud bricks. When it rained, much of this mud and clay from the homes was washed into the street. Little by little, the street level got higher. Sometimes the houses needed repair. Instead of repairing them, it was easier to build them over again. New houses were built where old ones had been. Over the years, the *tels* grew higher and higher.

When new houses were built over old ones, many objects were often buried in the remains of the old houses. Such things as dishes, toys, jewelry, tools, and clay tablets were left in the ruins. As time passed, many of these objects were broken or crushed.

● Why do you think the people of Mesopotamia rebuilt their cities on the same spots for several thousand years?

Many archaeologists went to Mesopotamia to dig into the *tels.* Life at the digging sites was very hard. Some of the archaeologists died. Many became very sick. Sometimes sandstorms would cover up weeks and weeks of work. Sometimes the archaeologists did not have enough money to stay in Mesopotamia for very long. The early archaeologists were able to dig through only the top layer of the *tels.*

A cross-section of an imaginary tel containing the ruins of three cities. Each city, or level, is shown by a different color. Level 3 is the oldest city in this tel. The passage of time, rains, and mud damaged or ruined many of the homes. Dirt was packed in around these ruins. New buildings (Level 2) were built on the crumbled remains of the first buildings. In time, the homes of Level 2 also had to be replaced. Another "new city" made up Level 1.

☐ Level 1   ☐ Level 2   ☐ Level 3

An artist's reconstruction of a house found in a Mesopotamian tel. Only part of the roof is shown so that you can see the inside. Made from mud bricks and clay, the house had rooms built around a central courtyard. They had windows as well as doors. Archaeologists know that many Sumerians lived in houses of this kind.

Some early archaeologists did overcome many of their problems, however. They found the remains of old buildings and temples. They found statues and tools. They also found thousands of clay tablets. Clay is a curious material. Out in the open, the rains will wear it away quickly. Yet, clay that is baked and buried under the earth can last for a very long time. The tablets found by the archaeologists were thousands of years old. They were covered with strange marks. These marks were the same kind of writing that the Italian had found on the bricks. The archaeologists thought the clay tablets must be the books of the ancient world!

The archaeologists still did not know about the Sumerians. They were still looking for the ancient civilizations described in the old stories. No one could read the cuneiform. The clay tablets continued to hold their secrets.

► If you wrote a note and threw it away, what would most likely happen to it? If a child who lived thousands of years ago wrote a note on clay, what might have happened to it?

● Why was the discovery of the clay tablets important? Why do we call the tablets "the books of the ancient world"?

The Fourth Clue: A Key to the Strange Writing

The cuneiform writing was different from any other writing known to man. No one knew how to *begin* to read it. The scholars needed another clue. Without it, they would never know what the writing said. This next clue was not found near the *tels*. It was not even found in Mesopotamia. The key to cuneiform writing was found in another part of the Middle East. It was found faraway in Persia (pėr′ zhə).

▶ Find Persia on the map on page 42. Then locate Persia on a modern map. What is Persia called today?

High in the mountains of Persia was a large rock. In ancient times, a Persian king had a message carved on this rock. He wanted everyone to know that he was a very great king. So he had the message carved in three different languages. All of these languages were written in cuneiform.

▶ Do you know of any languages today that share the same letters? Explain.

The rock was 300 feet above the ground. Archaeologists had not been able to get near it. One man who was interested in cuneiform figured out a way. To reach the rock, he used long ladders, cables, and hooks. Then, while he was dangling from the end of a rope, he copied the writing. Scholars now had a copy of the three messages. But what did the messages say? The greatest and hardest work still lay ahead. The scholars had to find out what the writing said.

One scholar had an idea. He knew that many writings of Persian kings began like this: "So-and-So, the great king, the king of kings, son of So-and-So. . . ." The scholar thought that maybe the cuneiform writing also began with these words. He studied the cuneiform to test his idea. The marks appeared in an order that told him he was right. He was able to read the first line! With this key, scholars could figure out one of the messages. It described the king's victories in battle, and how he had gained his throne. Then they used that message as a key to read the other two messages. One of these two messages was written in the language of ancient Babylonia.

The mysteries of cuneiform were solved when the characters on this rock were translated. Darius, the great Persian king, also had statues carved into the rock face. They show Darius claiming prisoners after a military victory.

Scholars matched the Babylonian message with the writing on the tablets from southern Mesopotamia. The cuneiform writing on the tablets did not match the writing of the Babylonians! That puzzled them. It made them suspect that the Babylonians had "borrowed" their writing from an earlier people.

► Can you guess whose writing the Babylonians had "borrowed"?

Step by step, the scholars had found the earliest writing of all. They learned how to read this writing. A whole new world opened up for them. The little clay tablets gave up their secrets. The tablets led the archaeologists back past the Babylonians to the people who had invented cuneiform writing. These people were the Sumerians. The mystery of Sumer was almost solved.

The Fifth Clue: Deeper Digging

It was the archaeologists who finally solved the mystery of Sumer. As they dug into the *tels* of southern Mesopotamia, they found

The work of an archaeologist takes a great deal of skill and patience. This man is trying to fit together fragments of pottery found among a city's ruins.

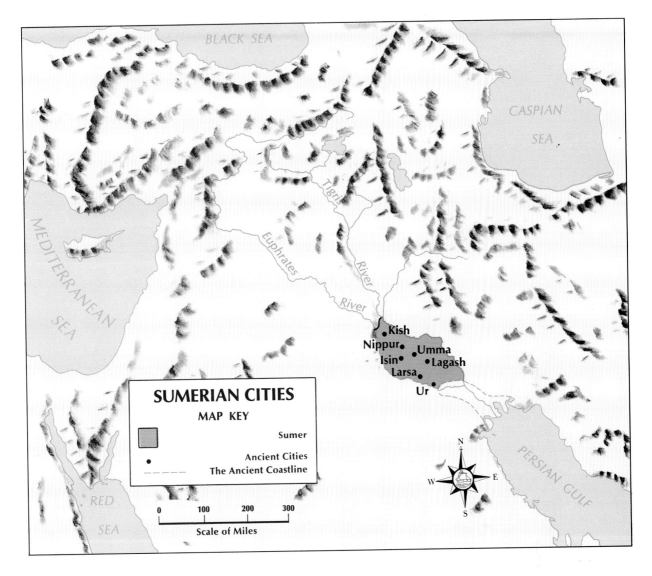

SUMERIAN CITIES

MAP KEY

Sumer

Ancient Cities

The Ancient Coastline

Scale of Miles

0   100   200   300

cities under cities. Then they found other cities under *those*. As they dug deeper and deeper, they found older and older things. They found some of the ancient cities of the Babylonians. Still, they kept on digging. At last they came to the cities of Sumer. The archaeologists then studied the Sumerian artifacts that they found. They were excited to find that these artifacts were made about 3500 B.C. People all over the world were amazed. Civilization in Mesopotamia was older than anyone had dreamed. The archaeologists had found remains from the earliest known civilization on earth.

★   Find out how archaeologists do their work. What tools do they use? How do they keep track of what they find?

Often, the archaeologists could not tell exactly what they had found. The artifacts had been buried for thousands of years. Many had been crushed by the weight of the earth on top of them. Sometimes they had been broken into many little pieces. These pieces were often mixed with dirt and clay. The archaeologists tried to remove the artifacts without breaking them into smaller pieces. Sometimes it took hours to remove a tiny piece of a single object!

- Look at the picture on page 69 of the harp with the bull's head as it was found by archaeologists. Look at the picture of the harp after it was restored. Describe the skills needed by an archaeologist.

- Why do you suppose archaeologists keep lists of what they find?

The archaeologists found many Sumerian treasures. They found helmets and gold crowns, gold drinking cups, daggers, harps, and silver jewelry. All these artifacts showed that the Sumerians had developed many special skills and talents. They also showed that the Sumerians had learned these things at a very early time.

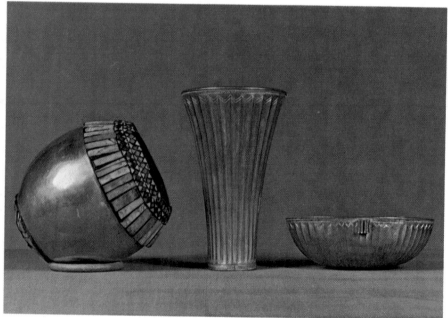

The Sumerians made many beautiful objects of gold. One of the most impressive pieces of the Sumerian craftsman is the golden goat, right. Found in a grave at Ur, this figure may have been used in religious ceremonies. The artist who made this figure used wood, gold, shells, and semiprecious stones in his design.

Why do you think this type of headpiece is often called a "wig helmet"?

Archaeologists learned much about the Sumerians from these two facts:

There were no metals or metal ores found in the earth around Sumer.

Objects made of metal were found in Sumerian cities.

- What do these two clues tell you about the Sumerians? How do you suppose the Sumerians got the metals?

What Happened Here?

Sir Leonard Woolley was a great archaeologist. He found the Sumerian city of Ur (èr). The map of Sumerian cities on page 51 shows where Ur was located. In 1925, Woolley made a discovery that excited the whole world. Deep under the city of Ur, he found a huge grave pit. At the bottom of the grave pit were the skeletons of many men and women. From the looks of the grave the people had all been buried on the same day. The body of one woman was set apart from the other bodies. She had been dressed more beautifully than the other women.

She wore a fancy headdress. Woolley called her Queen Shubad. He believed that the people buried with her were the members of her court.

★ The city of Ur is mentioned in the Book of Genesis in the Old Testament. Try to find out what is said about this city.

Woolley found many things lying in the grave pit. In one part, he found the skeletons of some Sumerian men. On their heads were copper helmets. At their sides were spears. They probably were the queen's soldiers. Woolley found the skeleton of one lady next to a harp. Her finger bones still lay across the strings of the harp. She must have been the court musician. Two wagons were found. The bones of oxen lay in front of them. In the wagons lay the bones of drivers. There were skeletons of 64 women in the grave pit. They were buried in wool dresses that had been bright red. They probably were ladies of the court.

All the skeletons were found in neat, orderly rows. There were no signs of any struggle or any violence. All the men and women in the grave pit must have died peacefully. What did it mean? Woolley studied the clues to find out. One particular clue seemed important. Next to each body was a little metal cup. Before you read on, think about the clues and see how much of the mystery you can solve for yourself.

After studying all the clues, Woolley gave his explanation of what-happened when Queen Shubad died. He believed that first, a large, deep hole was dug in the ground. Queen Shubad's body was placed in the grave pit. Then all the queen's servants climbed into the pit. They knew they were going to die. When they were all in the pit, each one drank from a cup. The cups probably held some kind of drug that put them to sleep. While they were asleep, the pit was filled with dirt. Then the funeral was over.

We will never know if Woolley's explanation was right. We do know that the grave pit was dug a very long time ago. Archaeologists have not found any other such grave pits in the remains from later periods of Sumer.

● Can you guess why the early rulers of Sumer were buried with many treasures? Why were their servants buried with them? Do you suppose the Sumerians believed in some kind of life after death?

The crushed and broken headdress of Queen Shubad. Lady Woolley was an archaeologist and an artist as well. She began to reconstruct the headdress. First, she had to carefully remove the many fragments from the ground.

- What can you tell about the work of the archaeologist from these pictures? What can you tell about Queen Shubad?

- Do you think archaeologists of the future will find out much about our civilization by digging up the graves of our important people? Why or why not?

A Mystery Is Solved

Even today, while we are studying Sumer, archaeologists are studying it, too. They are still digging into the *tels* in the land between the rivers. They are still learning more about the life of

The result of Lady Woolley's work is shown above. The head is a wax model of the skull of a Sumerian woman found in the death pit. The skull of Queen Shubad could not be used because it was too badly crushed.

the Sumerians. Archaeologists are also trying to learn more about other ancient peoples. It is even possible that they will discover a civilization which developed earlier than Sumer. However, one great mystery has been solved. Sumerian civilization—forgotten for nearly 4,000 years—has been identified.

● Is it possible that we might be forgotten the way the Sumerians were forgotten? Why or why not?

★ Suppose we were forgotten! Write a story about an archaeologist in A.D. 7000. Pretend that he is digging up your community. What things would he find? How would he use these things to try to describe our way of life? What kinds of things might puzzle him?

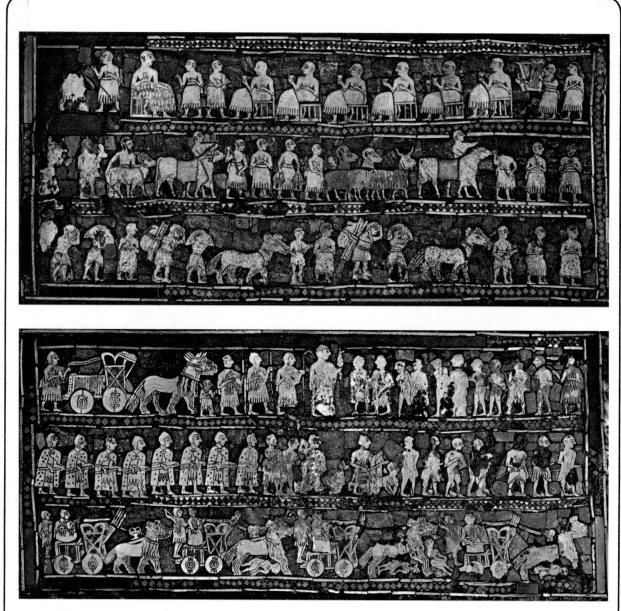

These two panels, made of wood, shells, and semiprecious stones, are known as the "Standard of Ur." They were found in a grave in the city of Ur. In the top panel, a king is holding a banquet. The other figures may be bringing gifts of animals, grain, and other goods to the king. The lower panel shows Sumerian soldiers fighting a battle and leading prisoners before their king. We can learn a great deal about such things as the Sumerians' appearance, their work, their skills, and their fighting methods from looking at the Standard. How much can you discover on your own?

and all the ideas they believe in. It includes their habits and customs, their religion and education, their art and music.

★ *Culture* includes all the things people learn in order to live in their society. Give some examples from your own culture. How did you learn them?

The chart on page 60 lists important questions to ask about culture. They are basic questions which can be used to study every culture. In this chapter, we will use the first two questions in our study of Sumerian culture. In later chapters, we will use the rest of the questions. Throughout *The Human Adventure*, we will be asking these same questions to study other cultures, including our own. Because these questions are so important, make sure that you understand all the words on the chart.

Now that you have read the questions, we are ready to begin our detective work on Sumerian culture. We know what questions to ask. Let's see if we can find the answers.

This drummer is a detail from a Sumerian vase. We can tell from artifacts like this that music was an important part of Sumerian culture.

How Did the Sumerians Change the Land?

The Sumerians learned to control the flooding of the Tigris and the Euphrates Rivers. They built earth walls, or levees, to hold back the waters of the spring floods. They dug canals to carry water to the fields during the long, hot summers.

The Sumerians learned how to work together. By helping one another, they were able to change their land. They were able to control their physical environment. Working together, the Sumerians created the world's first civilization.

The Sumerian Economy

People who lived before the Sumerians found that the division of labor was a good idea. Even the early food-gatherers divided the work. The women looked after the children and searched for vegetables. The men did the hunting and fishing.

The Sumerians went much further than the food-gatherers. They carried the division of labor further than any group had

Division of labor became very important to the Sumerian economy. What kind of work do you think this man did?

before. Let us see how they did this. Then we will know what their *economic* life was like. We will find out by asking the questions on economy on the chart on page 60.

How Did the Sumerians Produce Their Food?

The Sumerians worked hard. The land was irrigated by teams of workers. The results were wonderful. The Sumerians grew large amounts of grain in the irrigated soil. For the first time in history, men produced a surplus of food.

► You have already read about the development of a surplus. What does *surplus* mean?

The surplus of grain kept increasing. Not every Sumerian had to be a farmer. Not every Sumerian had to spend all his time producing food. Some of the people were able to grow enough food for all of the people.

The rest of the Sumerians were free to work at other jobs.

Fishermen found a plentiful supply of fish in the Tigris and Euphrates Rivers. Other men brought surplus food into the city from the farms.

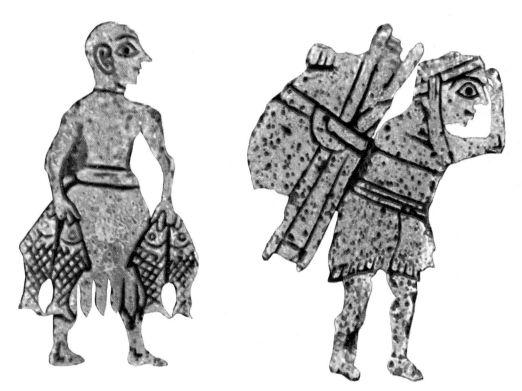

Some Sumerians became craftsmen, such as carpenters or metalworkers. Some made cloth. Some became priests, soldiers, or doctors. Some became cattle raisers, sheep herders, merchants, boatmen, or writers. All these people were able to eat by exchanging their goods or their services for grain and other kinds of food.

All these people lived together in cities or near cities. The cities were protected by high walls. Rich fields of wheat and barley stretched around the cities. In the fields, the farmers produced food for themselves and for the city people.

This relief of work in a dairy is another example of division of labor in Sumer. The man on the left is churning butter, while the next group of men seem to be straining milk into larger containers. On the right, a cow is being milked.

- What three things are necessary for civilization? Had the Sumerians become civilized?

- Who can produce more goods
      many people working at many different jobs, or
      each person trying to produce everything for himself? Explain.

- Why does the division of labor help to produce a surplus of goods? Why might it produce better goods than before?

- What can men do with a surplus of goods?

- How does a surplus of goods lead to *savings*? How do savings become *capital*?

- *Capital goods* are *goods used to produce other goods*. Name some capital goods of Sumer. What are *consumer goods*? Name some consumer goods in Sumer.

● Why did the craftsmen and other specialists live together in cities? If everyone lived in one place, might it be easier to transport and exchange goods? Might it be helpful for defense? Explain.

How Did the Sumerians Trade?

The land of Sumer had rich soil. It had water for irrigation. It had a long, hot growing season. However, there were many things it did not have. There was no timber in Sumer. There was no stone. There were no metals. The Sumerians needed and wanted all these things. Slowly, over many centuries, they learned that they could get them through trade.

The Sumerians had a surplus of grain and cloth. By this time, other societies had also developed civilizations. They wanted some of this grain and cloth. The Sumerians learned that they could trade their surplus for the things they needed.

It took many centuries for trade to develop between the Sumerians and other peoples. During these centuries, the Sumerians learned how to transport goods over long distances. They invented the wheel. By making carts and wagons, they were able to transport goods over land. By inventing the sailboat, they were able to transport goods on the rivers and on the sea.

The model of a sailboat was found in a child's grave. The four-wheeled Sumerian cart is also a model. Both were probably toys.

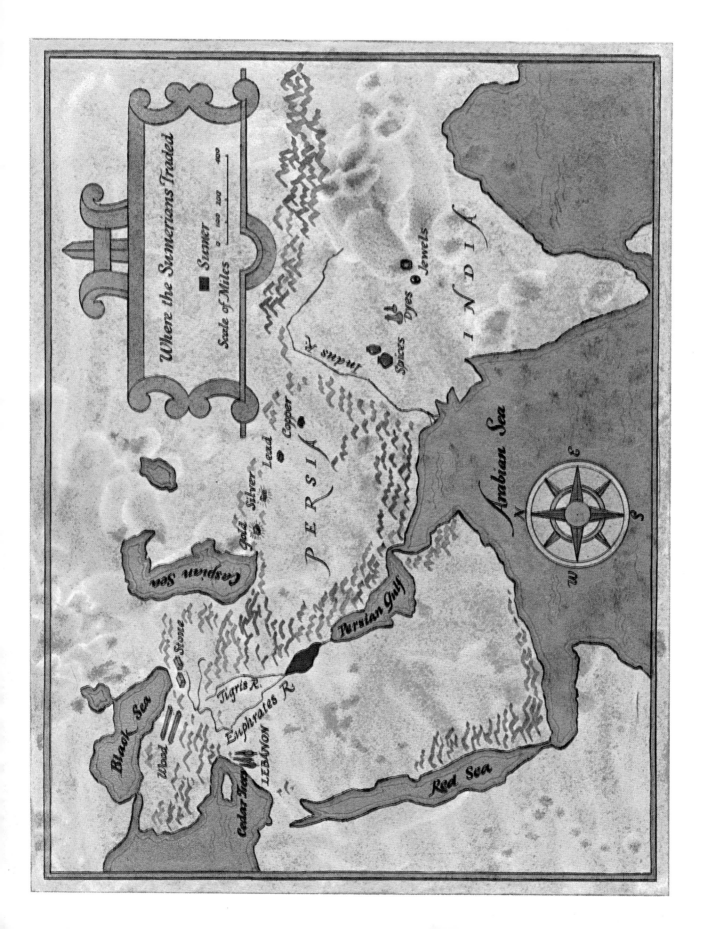

Where the Sumerians Traded

■ Sumer
Scale of Miles
0   100   200   400

INDIA

Jewels
Dyes
Spices

Indus R.

PERSIA

Copper
Lead
Silver
Gold

Caspian Sea

Arabian Sea

N
E
W
S

Persian Gulf

Stone

Tigris R.

Euphrates R.

Black Sea

Wood

Cedar Forest

LEBANON

Red Sea

Sumerian merchants brought stone and wood down the Tigris and Euphrates Rivers from the northern mountains. Cedar wood came from Lebanon. Gold, silver, lead, and copper came from Persia and other countries to the east. In later centuries, some Sumerian merchants may have traveled as far as India. There they could buy spices, dyes, and jewels.

The Sumerians found many uses for their new materials. New crafts developed. Some men learned how to make objects out of copper and bronze. Some learned how to carve wood. Others learned how to carve stone. The craftsmen made statues and tools out of their new materials. They made weapons and armor, jewelry and furniture. Archaeologists today have found many of the things made by the craftsmen of Sumer. Throughout this book, you will find pictures of some of these artifacts.

▶ Find the Sumerian trading places on the map on page 66. How did the Sumerian merchants get to each of them?

▶ What did the Sumerians trade for all the products they obtained?

● How would you explain the difference between a *necessity* and a *luxury*? Were the products traded for by the Sumerians necessities or luxuries?

▶ Is the automobile a necessity or a luxury in the United States? Is it a necessity or a luxury in India?

Transporting goods by water continued to be important long after the Sumerians. Centuries later, other civilizations also used the rivers for transportation and trade. This relief was made in the ninth century B.C.

Examples of Sumerian crafts. The golden doe, above, is less than two inches high and two inches long. Left, a statue of a lion-headed monster. Below, two wrestlers form the base of a copper vase.

Harp with a bull's head as found in the ground and the harp after it was restored

Close-up of a bull's head from a harp very much like the one above. Archaeologists restored it to this beautiful condition.

Did the Sumerians Use Money?

Barter was the earliest form of trading. **Barter** means that two people exchange goods or services without using any money. For example, Tom gives his pen to John for three baseball cards. Jane trades Mary a French postage stamp for a photo of a movie star.

Barter is not used very often today. In most societies, trading is done by means of money. Money is a **medium of exchange**. Money is something that anyone can take in exchange for goods or work. Anyone can use the money to buy something he wants.

● Why is money necessary when there is a wide division of labor? What would happen if your teacher had to go to each parent for payment for her services? She might get a book from one, a dress from another, a free bus ride from another, and so on.

The Sumerians needed a medium of exchange. Their merchants needed to find something that could be used as payment everywhere. For a time, they used barley, which is a grain. They learned that almost everyone would take barley in exchange for goods. The Sumerians paid their workers in barley. They baked their bread and brewed their beer from barley. The merchants used the surplus barley to trade for things they wanted.

Barley was not a very good medium of exchange, however. Large amounts of it were heavy. If the barley was not carefully stored, it could spoil. It was hard to handle. It was hard to transport over long distances. The Sumerian merchants wanted to find a better medium of exchange.

The Sumerian merchants found that silver would be accepted almost everywhere. As a medium of exchange, silver was better than barley. It was easier to use. It was easier to carry, and it did not spoil. It did not take up much room.

Silver was valuable because it was a precious metal. It was precious because it was scarce. The Sumerians weighed out the silver as they needed it. Later, they began to use small bars of silver. Each bar had a stamp that showed its weight. These bars of silver were the first metal money.

▶ Why was silver a better medium of exchange than barley?

▶ Is all our money today made of precious materials?

★ Why do we use mostly paper money today? What gives value to paper money?

How Did the Sumerians Distribute Their Goods?

The Sumerians had more than enough food for everyone. The surplus was used in trade. It brought wealth. It gave the Sumerians capital.

This wealth was not divided equally, however. In Sumer there were some rich people. There were also many poor people. The poor people were mainly the agricultural workers. They produced the surplus, yet they had just enough food to stay alive. There were also slaves in Sumer. Like the poor people, they had to work very hard. Out of every 100 men and women in Sumer, between 80 and 90 were agricultural workers. The workers and slaves helped to make the division of labor—and civilization—

Sumerian priests received a greater share of the surplus wealth than the agricultural workers.

possible. They produced the surplus necessary for civilization to develop. But the workers were not able to share in the new things that civilization brought.

● Suppose the surplus was shared equally every year. Would it be used up, or *consumed*? Could capital be saved up? How?

● Why did early civilization depend on a large group of poor people? Why can a civilized country like the United States exist today without depending on poor farmers?

★ How many people in India out of 100 must work as farmers? In the United States? Why are the figures so different?

In a *civilized economy* four things are necessary. These are land (or raw materials), capital, the work force, and managers. We have already studied the land in Sumer. It was just right for irrigated agriculture. We have also seen how capital came into being. The irrigation canals were capital goods. The cities, with their workshops, marketplaces, and other buildings, were capital goods. So were the trading ships. The farmers were the work force of the Sumerian economy. Now, who were the managers?

The managers were those people who directed the work. The managers also decided how to use capital. A civilized economy is not simple. Fields had to be plowed and planted and watered. Canals had to be dug and mended. Workers had to be given jobs.

Someone had to make plans. Someone had to decide how the water should be divided among the fields. Someone had to know when the spring floods would come. Certain men came to know these important things. They developed authority over the others. Their power grew. They were the managers.

The people who knew these important things were the priests of Sumer. The priests had many skills. They knew how to figure out the seasons. They knew the right time for planting. They knew how to lay out the canals. The priests became very powerful. Their power became even stronger because of Sumerian ideas about the gods. In the next chapter, we will learn about some of these ideas. We will be able to understand why the farm workers accepted their lower position, and allowed the priests to rule them.

● How do you think that the product was distributed among labor, capital, and management? Why would some groups have more consumer goods and services for each person than other groups? Which group would control the making of capital goods?

● How did the priests and their helpers get and keep their power?

EARLY SUMERIAN ECONOMY

THE FOUR THINGS NEEDED FOR PRODUCTION

Labor	Land and Raw Materials	Capital	Managers
farm workers canal diggers other workers	flood plains seed herds of animals imported wood stone metal etc.	canals levees stone-houses workshops ships carts tools etc.	priests their helpers

GOODS AND SERVICES

Capital Goods	Consumer Goods	Services
Surplus used to build and repair capital goods	food clothing shelter	transport personal service education etc.

chapter 4

What the Sumerians Believed and What They Knew

The Sumerians had learned to control their physical environment. Still there were many things that they could not control. There were many things they could not understand. These things filled them with fear and wonder.

Sometimes the river floods were very violent. Then towns and walls and canals were washed away. The floods were a **force of nature**. They filled the Sumerians with fear. The Sumerians could not stop the floods, and they could not understand what caused them.

The Sumerians had many questions and fears about other forces of nature—the rain, the wind, and the sun. They did not know why the rain fell. They did not know why the wind blew. They did not know why the sun rose and set. They did know, however, that they could not control any of these forces of nature.

▶ Name some other forces of nature that might have filled the Sumerians with fear and wonder.

What Did the Sumerians Believe About the Gods?

The Sumerians had no way of finding scientific answers to these mysteries. They solved the mysteries in their own way. They decided that all the forces of nature were alive. A clap of thunder was alive. The sun was alive. The rain and wind were alive. The Sumerians began to worship many of the forces of nature. They began to worship the god of the sun. They began to worship the god of the rain. Every natural force was a god. Their whole world became filled with gods!

Let us read a Sumerian story. From this story we will learn what the Sumerians thought about the power of the gods.

THE SUMERIAN STORY OF THE GREAT FLOOD

In those days there were many, many people. The people made so much noise that the gods could not sleep. So the gods decided to destroy mankind. They decided to send a flood to cover the earth.

One god felt sorry for mankind. He decided to warn one good man that the flood was coming. He told the good man to tear down his house and build a boat. The good man listened to the words of the god. He built a boat, and into it he loaded all of his possessions. He loaded all his family and all his relatives. He loaded all the animals of the fields, both wild and tame, and all the craftsmen.

Then a black cloud arose in the sky. All that was bright turned into darkness. The rains came and the winds blew. Even the gods were frightened by what they had done. For six days and six nights, the flood marched over the earth and waged war like an army. Then, on the seventh day, the sea grew calm. The flood was stilled.

The good man looked out at the world from his boat. All was silent. He could find no land. He could see only water. All mankind had turned to mud! He sat down and cried.

Then a mountain appeared in the distance. The boat moved toward the mountain and was grounded on it. The boat would not budge. The good man set loose a dove. The dove flew away but found no resting place because the waters had not gone down. It returned. Later the man set loose a swallow. The swallow flew away but found no resting place. It, too, returned. Finally the man set loose a crow. The crow saw that the waters had gone down. It ate and flew around and cawed. It did not return.

Then the sun god came out and warmed the earth. The good man gave thanks that he was alive. He bowed before the sun god and offered sacrifices of oxen and sheep. Because he was so good, he was given eternal life by the gods.

▶ What Old Testament story tells of a great flood sent to destroy mankind?

▶ Who is the hero of this Bible flood story? How did he survive?

● Can you guess which story is more ancient—the Bible story or the Sumerian story? What reasons can you give?

● What clues in the story tell you that the Sumerians were afraid of the power of the gods?

Sumerian artists often illustrated stories about the gods and important events. These animal scenes may have been illustrations of a Sumerian legend.

● Give some other reasons why the Sumerians would be afraid of the gods. (Clue: Did the Sumerians depend on the yearly floods? What would happen if the floods were too violent? What would happen if they were too low?)

★ Read the story of the flood in the Bible. How does this story explain the reason for the flood? What differences can you find between the idea of God in the Bible and the idea of the gods in the Sumerian story?

The Sumerians believed that the gods controlled everything. If the gods were happy, men would be happy. If the gods were angry, the whole world might fall apart! The gods could easily change their minds. One moment they might be happy. The next moment they might be very angry. Anything the gods wanted to do was done. That was how the world had been created!

THE SUMERIAN STORY OF THE CREATION OF THE WORLD

Once there was only endless sea. From this sea a mountain grew. The mountain was heaven and earth joined together. The god of heaven and the goddess of the earth gave birth to a son. His name was Enlil, and he was god of the air. Enlil separated heaven and earth. Heaven became the sky and the "great above." Earth became the land and the "great below." They were separated by air.

This woodcut of the sun god was copied from a Sumerian artifact.

But the world was still in darkness. Enlil was caught in the darkness and did not like it. So he and his wife gave birth to the moon. The moon god traveled in a boat bringing light to the dark blue sky. Around the moon the "little ones" (the stars) were scattered like grain. Around the moon the "big ones" (the planets) walked like wild oxen.

Still it was dark during the day. So the moon god and his wife gave birth to the sun god. The sun god rose in the mountain of the east and set in the mountain of the west. The world was bright.

▶ What other story do you know that tells how the world was created?

★ Read the story of the creation of the world in the Bible. In what ways is this story of creation like the Sumerian story? In what ways is it different?

▶ Can you tell which story is more ancient?

The Sumerians carved statues of the gods from stone. From the statues we can see what they thought the gods looked like. Many gods looked like short people with round bellies. They had thin lips and big noses. They wore skirts made of sheep's wool. In fact, many statues of the gods looked like the statues the Sumerians made of themselves!

What Did the Sumerians Believe About the Meaning of Their Lives?

The gods of Sumer looked like men—and they acted like men. The gods liked good food and nice clothing. They got married and had children. Sometimes they were kind. Sometimes they were cruel. Either way, the Sumerians believed they had no control over what the gods did. Rather, the Sumerians believed that they were slaves of the gods. This story tells why.

THE SUMERIAN STORY OF THE CREATION OF MAN

The gods had always worked for a living. But when the goddesses were created, the gods had to work even harder to keep them happy. Then the gods had great trouble getting enough bread to eat and enough clothing to wear. They got angry. They wanted servants who would take care of their needs. So they took some clay and made it thick. They shaped the clay until arms and legs appeared, and then they gave the clay life. Thus was man made from river mud and given life by the gods. Men were placed on earth as servants of the gods. They gave food, clothing, and shelter to the gods. They set the gods free from ever having to work again.

▶   What other story do you know that tells how man was created?

★   Read the story of man's creation in the Bible. In what ways is this Bible story like the Sumerian story? In what ways is it different?

●   What did the Sumerians believe about the meaning of their lives? Use clues from the story to explain your answer.

Being the slaves of the gods was not easy for the Sumerians. They had to do everything possible to keep the gods happy. How did they know what would please the gods? They did not know. Only the priests knew. Only the priests could talk to the gods and learn what would please them. The priests were the representatives of the gods on earth.

The Sumerians obeyed the priests. By obeying them, they thought they were obeying the gods. So the priests were able to make the Sumerians work hard and long. The priests told the workers when to plant and when to harvest. They told them when to dig canals and when to build earth walls. They told them when to make war and when to make peace. Without the priests, the first civilization might never have come into being!

Each Sumerian city had its own special god. The Sumerians in each city believed that one special god owned the city, the land, and the people. The priests of the city ruled in place of this god. To honor the god the priests made the people build a temple. It was the largest and most important building in a Sumerian city. It rose above the city like a hill. Such a hill temple was called a **ziggurat** (zig′ ŭ rat′). The ziggurat was the "mountain of god." It was the "hill of heaven." Here is an Old Testament story that tells about plans to build a tower. The tower may have been a ziggurat.

THE STORY OF THE BUILDING OF THE TOWER

Now the whole world had one language. And as men traveled in the east, they found a plain in the land of Shinar (Sumer) and settled there. And they said to one another, "Come, let us make bricks, and burn them well." So they used bricks for stone, and slime for mortar. Then they said, "Come, let us build ourselves a city with a tower whose top shall reach the heavens."

► Look at the drawing below and the photograph on the next page. What materials were used to build a ziggurat? What shape did it have?

An artist's reconstruction of a ziggurat. The ziggurat was built with several levels, or terraces. There were three huge stairways, one in the center and one at each side. Processions of priests climbed the central stairway to the temple at the top. Notice how tiny the figures of people on the stairways appear.

Within a city, all life centered on the ziggurat of the special city god. The Sumerians believed that the god lived on top of the ziggurat. Three times a day the priests brought food to the god. Only the priests could enter the room where the god lived.

The farm workers worked in the fields of the god. Then they brought the surplus grain to the temple of the city god. In return, the city god protected them and the city from harm. The Sumerian idea of life is shown on page 83.

▶ Was religion an important part of Sumerian life?

● What effect did religious ideas have upon these five things?
    how the Sumerians were governed
    how the land was farmed
    who owned the land
    how surplus grain was divided
    what the Sumerians thought about themselves

This view of the ruins of the ziggurat of Ur shows the left-hand stairway. You can see the clay bricks with which the temple was built.

SUMERIAN IDEA OF LIFE

THE GODS

FORCES OF NATURE

PRIESTS who understand the gods

MEN who were slaves of the gods

What New Knowledge Did the Sumerians Develop?

We have already seen how the Sumerians slowly developed a surplus of food and a division of labor. A division of labor meant that people became specialists. Some people continued to farm the land. Others built houses, made tools, or worked at one of many other jobs. Some people did work that used their minds more than their hands. They had time to think about life in Sumer. They had time to develop new ideas and new ways of solving problems. Let us read about some examples of new knowledge developed by the Sumerians.

New Knowledge – Arithmetic

The priests of Sumer had to keep track of many important things. How much land was being farmed? How much surplus grain was in the temple? How much grain should be given to the workers?

The merchants of Sumer also had to keep track of their business matters. How much grain had they sold? What price did they get for the grain? How much stone or copper could they buy?

To keep track of these things, the Sumerians invented signs to represent numbers. They used these signs to develop a system of arithmetic. Their system was based on two numerals.

► Look at the diagram below. Find the Sumerian numerals for 1 and for 60. What do you notice about them?

Sumerian numerals. Can you understand the arithmetic problem at the bottom of the page?

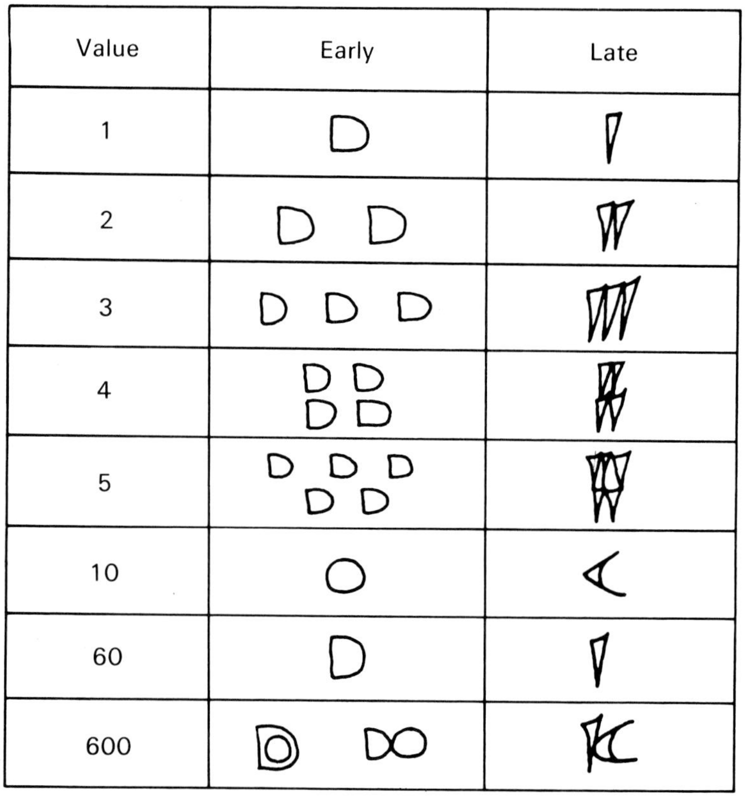
Value
Early
Late
1
2
3
4
5
10
60
600

= 600 + 60 x 4 + 10 + 5 = 855

It is not hard to see why the Sumerians chose 10 for one of their numerals. Most men have used 10 as a base for counting. That is because most men learned to count by using the 10 fingers on their two hands.

▶ What base do we use today for our decimal system of numeration?

Almost any other number besides 10 can be used as a base for counting. The Sumerians chose to use 60, along with 10. Base 60 helped them in their measurement of time and circles. Today our system of arithmetic is different from the Sumerian system. However, we still use some ideas developed by the Sumerians. One example is the way in which we measure circles. We divide the circumference of a circle into 360 degrees ($= 6 \times 60$).

● How do we use 60 to measure time?

★ Find out how to measure angles with a protractor. What do we call an angle of 90 degrees? What does an angle of 180 degrees look like?

New Knowledge—Sumerian Writing

The priests and merchants of Sumer also wanted to keep records of *what goods they had, what goods they bought,* and *what goods they sold.* In time, this led them to develop the world's first system of writing.

No Sumerian ever sat down and said, "Now I am going to write." Writing was invented slowly. It took hundreds of years to develop. Picture writing was the first step. The Sumerian priests began to write by drawing pictures of objects. They drew pictures of cows and sheep. They drew pictures of hands and feet. They drew pictures of stars and of many other things.

As time went on, some of the pictures began to stand for more than one thing. A picture of a foot might also mean "to stand," "to walk," or "to run." A picture of a star might also mean "the sky," "the heavens," or "the gods." This way of writing was confusing. The same picture could mean many different things. This way of writing was also difficult. What picture could the priests use to stand for "truth," "justice," or "courage"?

Objects	Early Picture Writing	Later Cuneiform Signs
Plow		
Boat (with Sails?)		
Chisel		
Axe		

The development of Sumerian writing from early picture writing to cuneiform

Slowly the Sumerian writing changed. Signs began to stand for *words*, not objects. Pictures changed into wedge-shaped marks. The Sumerians were able to put the wedge-shaped marks together in a series. Then they could write sentences as well as words.

▶ What is this wedge-shaped writing called?

Tablets showing early picture writing and later cuneiform signs

One more change took place in Sumerian writing. Some of the wedge-shaped marks began to stand for sounds instead of ideas or objects. A special mark would stand for each sound in the Sumerian language. Then, each time someone needed to write a word with a certain sound in it, he used the wedge-shaped mark that stood for the sound.

- Why was it a great step forward when signs began to stand for words and sounds instead of objects?

- Why was it a great step forward when the Sumerians could write sentences?

The Sumerians wrote with reeds that were hard and sharp and pointed. They wrote by pressing the reed into a tablet of soft clay. Each time they pressed a reed into the clay, it left a wedge-shaped mark. When they finished writing, they baked the tablet in the hot sun or in an oven so that it would harden.

This tablet was found in a Sumerian temple. It is an example of early cuneiform. The drawing on the right will help you to pick out the cuneiform signs.

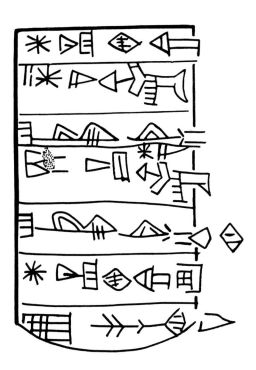

A Sumerian scribe, or writer. Since many Sumerians did not know how to write, a scribe's skill was very important.

Writing on Tablets and Cylinder Seals

Writing was an important invention. It was too important for the Sumerians to keep to themselves. As their trade grew, the Sumerians sent more than products out of their country. They sent ideas, too. Sumerian writing spread to many parts of the Middle East.

- Why is writing so important? Name some ways in which writing affects your life today.

- How would writing help the growth of business and trade in Sumer?

Writing on tablets was far from easy. Only a few Sumerians knew how to do it. Yet many Sumerians were engaged in business and trade. Every big business deal had to be put in writing. Then the writing had to be signed by the people who were making the deal. So the Sumerians invented the **cylinder seal.** They used the cylinder seal as a *signature.* They used it to sign their names.

A cylinder seal and its "signature"

The cylinder seals were made of clay or stone. Every important Sumerian had his own cylinder seal. He usually carried it around his neck. A different picture or design was carved on every seal. When a person had to sign his name on a tablet, he rolled his cylinder over the wet clay. The picture or design stayed on the clay. The picture was his signature.

Thousands of Sumerian tablets have been found by archaeologists. Most of these tablets deal with business matters. Only a small number of the tablets contain stories or poetry.

Which of these cylinder seals made the signature shown in the bottom picture?

Archaeologists have learned many things about the knowledge and economic life of the Sumerians from reading tablets about business and trade. They have also learned a great deal about the Sumerians and their beliefs by reading the tablets containing stories and poetry.

One such tablet tells about the adventures of a Sumerian hero. His name was Gilgamesh (gil′gə mesh′). Gilgamesh was strong and mighty. He was the first "superman." The story of Gilgamesh and his adventures was written as a very long poem. Let us read one story from the tablet about Gilgamesh. As you read, you will learn something about the kind of hero the Sumerians admired.

A STORY OF GILGAMESH

Gilgamesh knew all things. He knew all the countries of the world. He was wise. He understood mysteries. He knew secret things. The great gods created Gilgamesh. They made him two-thirds god and one-third man. They made his body perfect. The sun god gave him beauty. The storm god gave him courage.

The gods decided that Gilgamesh should have a friend. So a goddess dipped her hands in the waters and pinched off some clay. Thus the noble Enkidu (en ki dū) was created.

Enkidu ate grass in the hills. He played with wild beasts at the water holes. He loved the company of herds of wild game. He

The hero, Gilgamesh

roamed over the hills with wild beasts, and he was happy. He was strong and brave. He was a match even for Gilgamesh. Mighty Gilgamesh and Enkidu met and fought each other. In fighting, they learned that each was as strong as the other. Then they became friends.

In those days evil lurked in the land. Gilgamesh tried to find the cause of the evil so he could destroy it. This is what he found.

In the forest of cedars lived an evil giant named Humbaba. No man ever went into the forest, for all men were afraid of Humbaba. Humbaba was the watchman of the forest. He never slept.

Enkidu warned Gilgamesh of all these things. But Gilgamesh decided to go to the forest and destroy the evil giant. Gilgamesh said to Enkidu, "Only the gods live forever. Since we are men, our days are numbered. Our cares are but a breath of wind." And so Gilgamesh and Enkidu went to the land of Humbaba.

When they got to the forest, Gilgamesh took an axe and began to chop down the trees. Humbaba heard the noise and he was very angry. He came out from his house of cedar. His face looked like a lion's. His teeth were like dragon's fangs. He charged at Gilgamesh and fixed on him the eye of death. Gilgamesh prayed to the gods for help.

The gods sent many winds to help Gilgamesh. They sent the great wind, the north wind, the whirlwind, the cold wind, and the dry wind. The winds beat against Humbaba until he could not move. Humbaba was frightened. He begged Gilgamesh to spare his life. He promised to serve Gilgamesh and make him lord of the forest.

Enkidu told Gilgamesh not to listen. Humbaba was evil, and was speaking evil words. He was trying to trick Gilgamesh. So Gilgamesh struck Humbaba. He fell and lay there, deathly still. Then confusion followed. The mountains were moved and the hills were moved. The watchman of the cedar lay dead. Evil was gone from the land.

What can you learn about the Sumerians from this story? Here are questions to help you.

- In what ways did the Sumerians depend on the gods? Did even the mighty Gilgamesh need the help of the gods?

- What did the Sumerians believe about right and wrong? Did they believe that good conquered evil? Was it always easy to be good?

chapter 5

How the Sumerians Lived

In this chapter we will read about everyday life in a Sumerian city. We will learn something about Sumerian government, laws, family life, and education.

How Were the Sumerians Governed?

Each Sumerian city had its god. Each had its own government. The people loved their city and were proud of it. They believed that they must defend it against any enemy. They were also proud of their city god and of their priests, who ruled as kings. These early rulers were called priest-kings. The diagram on page 94, which pictures priestly rule in Sumer, shows the kind of power they had.

Sometimes the different cities of Sumer disagreed. Then the priest-kings might decide to go to war. However, they did not always decide such important matters on their own. Sometimes they called a meeting of all free men. These meetings were known as **assemblies**. In the assemblies, all the free men of Sumer were able to have a vote and have a voice in their government. Slaves had no voice in the assemblies. Neither did women and children.

● What does *patriotism* mean? Were the Sumerians patriotic? Explain.

Slowly, during many centuries, the Sumerians developed a set of written laws. They were the first people in history to write down their laws. They had laws about almost everything they did.

● Why does a civilized society need a set of written laws?

● What can happen if people do not write down their laws?

PRIESTLY RULE IN SUMER

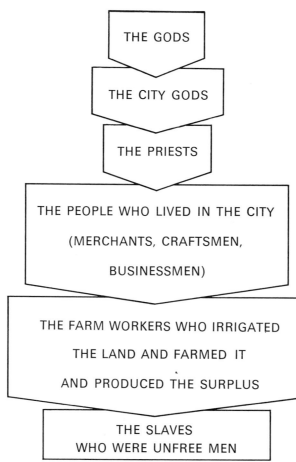

THE GODS

THE CITY GODS

THE PRIESTS

THE PEOPLE WHO LIVED IN THE CITY

(MERCHANTS, CRAFTSMEN,

BUSINESSMEN)

THE FARM WORKERS WHO IRRIGATED

THE LAND AND FARMED IT

AND PRODUCED THE SURPLUS

THE SLAVES
WHO WERE UNFREE MEN

This stone slab shows how the priest-kings got their power. On the top two levels the priest-king is receiving power from the gods. Most of the other levels are in fragments. They probably showed the priest-king leading his people. In this way he would be serving the gods. The ladder may have shown the people building a ziggurat to honor the gods.

What Kind of Laws Did the Sumerians Have?

Sumerian law tried very hard to protect those people who could not always take care of themselves. Here are some laws from the later years of Sumerian civilization:

Widows and orphans could not be taxed.

A father had to support his children and the mother of his children.

Slavery was legal, but slaves had certain rights. Slaves could own land. They could carry on business. They could appeal to the courts if they were being sold to a master they did not like. They could even buy their freedom. Still, slaves were the property of their owner. They could be bought and sold. A grown man could be bought for much less than the price of a donkey! For certain crimes, free men could be made slaves.

The Sumerian laws set down all the crimes for which people could be punished. They also named the punishment.

A king of the Sumerian city of Lagash

By 2000 B.C., the Sumerians had kinder laws than some of the people who lived long after them. Ancient peoples who lived after the Sumerians often demanded cruel punishment for crimes. Their laws would demand punishment of "an eye for an eye" and "a tooth for a tooth." For example, suppose a man poked out the eye of another man. Then his own eye would have to be poked out in punishment. For many crimes in Sumer, a person did not have to face such cruel physical punishment. Instead, he had to pay a money fine. Here is one such law:

> If a man bites the nose of another man and harms it, he shall pay a certain amount of silver. If he harms the eye of another man, he shall pay a certain amount of silver. For a tooth, he shall pay 1/2 that amount of silver. For an ear, he shall pay 1/2 the amount of silver. If he slaps another man in the face, he shall pay 1/10 the amount of silver.

● What is the meaning of the punishment, "an eye for an eye" and "a tooth for a tooth?"

● In what ways were the laws of Sumer like our laws? In what ways were they different?

Most of the time Sumerian laws were fair and just. Still there were times when unjust men made the laws. Then there was trouble in the land. Let us read a story that tells about such a time. The story was written on one of the clay tablets of Sumer.

THE TIME OF TROUBLE

During a war some men built up great power. They took donkeys from the people. They took sheep, fish, and grain from them. Taxes went higher and higher. Yet nobody minded, for all these things happened during time of war.

When the war ended, the men would not give up their power. They had become very rich, and they wanted to get richer. So they kept taking from the people and sent many people to jail. There were tax collectors from one end of the land to the other.

Sumerian soldiers going off to war. They wear helmets and carry spears.

The rulers got fatter and richer. Everything belonged to them. The people got thinner and poorer. They had to beg for their food. During this hard time a new ruler was chosen by the god of the city. He was a good man. Once again, he set up the laws of the god.

The good man carried out all the commands of the god. He freed all the people who were in jail. He gave them back their property. He gave the temple back to its real owner, the god of the city. The poor no longer suffered. There were no longer any wicked tax collectors in the land.

- Why did no one mind that certain men had great powers during wartime? Why did they mind when the war was over?

- Did the Sumerians have great respect for the law? What parts of the story help you to answer this question?

Did the Sumerians Live in Family Groups?

Most Sumerians lived in families. A family was made up of a husband, his wife, and their children. Sumerian law said that a man could have only one wife.

The husband was the head of the household. If he was poor, he always had one way to pay his debts. He could sell his wife and children as slaves for as long as three years! Still, a Sumerian woman did have some rights under the law. She could own property and could carry on business. She could own slaves and sell slaves. She could be a witness in a court of law. When her husband went away, she could run his affairs, unless she had grown-up sons who could take care of these things.

A bronze frying pan from a Sumerian household of more than 4,000 years ago

Sumerian children had to obey *all* the older members of their family. The children had to obey their parents in everything. They also had to obey their older brothers and sisters. If the children made their parents angry, they could be sent to another city. They could even be sold as slaves! Parents also arranged marriages for their children. The marriage took place when a clay marriage tablet was made and signed before witnesses.

As you can see, parents had complete control over their children. Still we must not think that Sumerian parents were unkind to their children. Most parents loved their children very much. They took good care of them. In return, the Sumerian children loved and obeyed their parents.

- Compare family life in Sumer with family life in your town. What things are the same? What things are different?

- Explain why you would, or would not, like to live in Sumer.

Fragment of a window grill from a Sumerian house

Did Sumerian Children Go to School?

The Sumerians had the first schools. Their schools were often in the temples. Only rich boys were able to attend them. The schools were called **edubbas** (ē dü bəs), or tablet houses. Their main purpose was to teach boys how to write. Most business deals had to be put in writing. The Sumerians needed people who could read and write.

Later, the Sumerian schools taught other subjects besides writing. In one course, students learned the names of plants and animals, and of stones and minerals. In another course, students learned how to work problems in arithmetic. The students also learned stories and poems of the past. They learned the poems by copying them on their tablets.

A Sumerian schoolboy practiced writing a god's name three times on this tablet.

Sumerian students did not have an easy life. They attended school from sunrise to sundown. They learned how to write by copying lines over and over on their tablets. There were no special activities. There was little or no class discussion. Work at the school seemed to be the same day after day.

The school principal was the **ummia** (ū mē ə) or "school father." There was also "a man in charge of the whip." He took care of the boys who disobeyed. The pupils were called the "school sons." The boys who graduated were called "school sons of days past."

Sumerian schoolboys were afraid to break the rules. Let us read a story about a school day in Sumer. The story is taken from a clay tablet.

A BAD DAY AT SCHOOL

Before going to bed, one schoolboy asked the family servants to wake him in time for class. However, they failed to wake him up, and he slept late. When he awakened, he jumped out of bed. He grabbed two rolls for lunch and ran all the way to school. Filled with fear, he entered the classroom and bowed low before his teacher. His low bow did not save him from a terrible day. First, he had been late. During the day, he forgot some lines in the lesson he wrote on his tablet. He also talked without permission. "The man in charge of the whip" beat him for all these things and also for breaking other school rules. But the boy had a rich father who invited the poorly paid teacher to dinner. The father gave the teacher new clothes, a ring for his finger, and many other gifts. After this visit to the boy's home, the teacher began to treat his student more kindly.

Children in ancient Sumer sometimes fought. One clay tablet tells how two boys insulted each other. Each boy said that the other did not know how to write or multiply correctly. They called each other insulting names, like "windbag" and "chatterbox" and "bully." Finally the principal came and put an end to the argument.

- Compare the Sumerian school with your school.

Ruins of a Sumerian schoolhouse reveal that students had to sit on hard benches during their long school day.

A lion-headed eagle spreads her wings over two deer. This powerful bird is seen often in Sumerian sculpture. She seems to have had importance in the religion of Sumer. This relief was found in a Sumerian temple.

What Have We Learned About Sumerian Culture?

In these last three chapters we have learned many things about Sumerian culture. Now let us think again about the chart on page 60, which lists questions to ask about a culture. The chart lists questions in seven, neat, orderly sets. We have found, however, that Sumerian culture did not always fall into such neat sets. For example, remember the Sumerian ideas about religion. Those ideas spread throughout the culture. Religion was very important to the Sumerians. It had great influence on all parts of Sumerian life.

When we studied Sumerian religion, we learned something about Sumerian *government*. Because of the importance of religion, the Sumerians were ruled by priest-kings.

When we studied Sumerian religion, we learned something about Sumerian *social groups*. Because of religious ideas, the priest-kings were at the top of Sumerian society.

When we studied Sumerian religion, we learned something about the Sumerian ideas of *art*. The Sumerians carved statues of the gods. They built ziggurats in honor of the gods.

Now, keeping these things in mind, turn back to the chart. See how many of the questions you can answer. Find out how good a detective you have been.

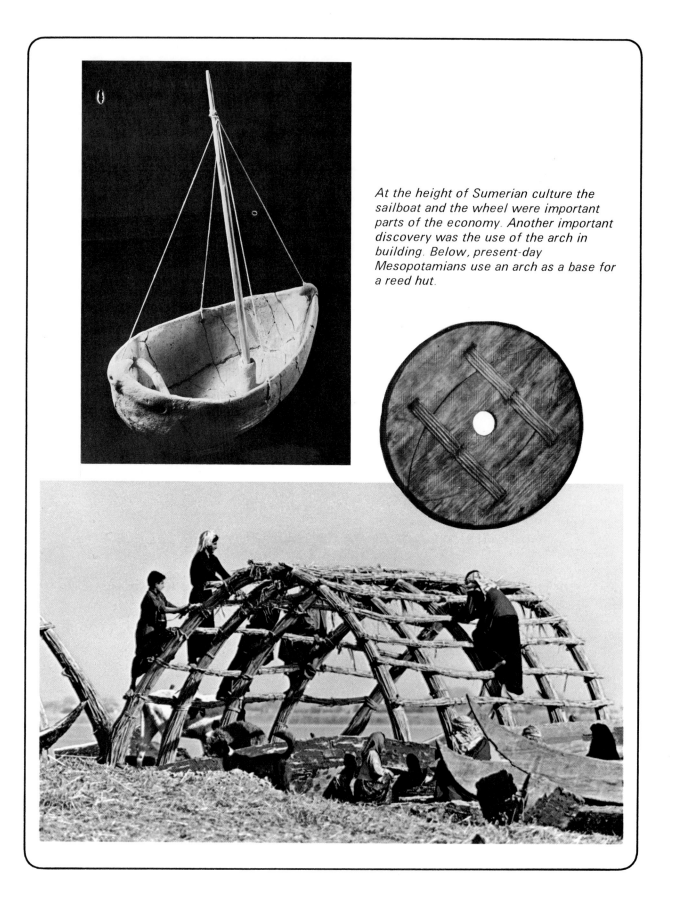

At the height of Sumerian culture the sailboat and the wheel were important parts of the economy. Another important discovery was the use of the arch in building. Below, present-day Mesopotamians use an arch as a base for a reed hut.

chapter 6

The Fall of Sumerian Culture

Sumerian culture reached its highest point during the third millennium B.C. After that, it lasted for about another thousand years. During those years many changes took place in Sumer. Sumerian culture slowly lost strength. By 1700 B.C., it could no longer be called Sumerian. Let us see how this great change came about.

Geographic Change in Sumer

Geographic change played a part in the downfall of Sumer. Over the years the Sumerians kept irrigating their land. Eventually, irrigation proved to be harmful. The water used for irrigation had salt in it. When the water evaporated, the salt would be left in the soil. Then crops would not grow. This change took place very slowly in Sumer. The Sumerians did not understand just why it was happening. The problem became serious between 2400 and 1700 B.C. In later centuries this geographic change harmed agriculture throughout the Middle East.

★ Try this experiment: Fill a clear glass about one-third full with tap water. Set it in the sun to let it evaporate. Repeat this process several times. Write down a description of the glass at the end of the experiment. What has happened?

The Rise of City-States

Political changes also played a part in the downfall of Sumer. When Sumer was young, the cities were quite small. There were stretches of swamp or desert land between the cities. Priest-kings from the temples in different cities often met together to share ideas.

Over the years the population grew and grew. So did the cities. More land was added to them. Swamps were drained. Desert land was irrigated and made to grow crops. The cities became **city-states**. A city-state is made up of the city itself plus the land around it. These two areas are under the same political control.

Soon the grainfields of one city-state bordered on those of another. The priest-kings of the various city-states had nowhere to get new land for growing crops. The Sumerians began to fight with each other. They fought over the boundaries of their land. They fought over water rights. The people in some city-states even built canals that led to fighting. These canals would bring water away from the fields of one city-state into the fields of another city-state.

The people in each city-state wanted their own city-state to be the most important of all. First one and then another city-state claimed to have power over all of Sumer. Wars broke out to see who was the strongest.

Even though wars broke out, Sumerian city-states were not well organized for war. They had no experience in fighting. The Sumerians had always thought their main duty was to please the gods by obeying the priest-kings, and by doing the work which they were asked to do. If they now had to fight wars, they would have to do things in a different way. They would need weapons, and they would need someone to lead them into battle.

The Rise of Military Kings

In the early days, the assembly of each city-state would put a military leader in charge whenever war broke out. The military leader was supposed to be in charge only as long as the war lasted. Every Sumerian man had to serve this leader as a soldier if he was asked to do so. Later on, however, these military leaders became kings. They remained kings even in times of peace. They passed on the kingship to their sons. The ruling power of the king's palace became stronger than the ruling power of the temple.

Why did the ruling power pass from the priest-kings to the military kings? Part of the answer is that military kings controlled the armies. That control gave them real power. The military kings also claimed that they were close to the gods, just as the priests were. They claimed to understand the gods just as well as the priest-kings did. So they claimed the right to rule for both military and religious reasons.

● Explain the drawing below in your own words.

The figures at the far left in this drawing are gods.

The wars between the city-states were long and hard. There were many bloody battles. The armies had soldiers who fought on foot. They had soldiers who fought from donkey-drawn carts. The soldiers wore copper helmets and leather kilts. They used spears and swords and shields.

After a battle with another city-state, the winning army would often kill all its prisoners. The king of one city-state boasted that in just one battle he killed 3,000 of the enemy. Some prisoners might be made slaves. Some might be held for ransom. Sometimes the captured city was robbed and destroyed. Then its temple would be knocked to the ground. That was the worst thing that could happen to a city-state. Destruction of the temple meant that its god had lost to the god of the winning city-state.

Over the years, kings of stronger city-states were able to bring several city-states together under their control. After 2375 B.C., the king of the city-state of Umma brought most Sumerian

A donkey-drawn war cart from the "Standard of Ur." You can see the leather kilts and copper helmets of the soldiers.

War played an important part in the history of the ancient Middle East. In this bronze relief, the enemy soldiers have set fire to the city and are preparing to climb the city's walls.

city-states under his control. When one ruler was able to gain power over many city-states, that was the beginning of the world's first **empire**. It did not last long, however. Soon fighting broke out again among the city-states.

▶ Find out what *empire* means.

● Might it have been a good thing for the Sumerian city-states to have joined together in one united empire? Why or why not?

The Coming of the Barbarians

The wars among the city-states were a great political problem of the Sumerians. They had another great problem, too. Around the edges of Sumer lived people who were not civilized. These people did not live in cities. Some were herdsmen who had settled down. Some were nomads who kept herds of animals. These people had a culture and a way of life of their own. However, they saw that civilization also had advantages. They wanted a share in some of the good things that civilization brought. Unfortunately for the Sumerians, these people sometimes helped themselves. They attacked and robbed Sumerian cities.

The kind of people we have just described are called **barbarians**. Barbarians are people who live on the edges of civilization. They are not civilized. Still they know about civilization and what it can offer. Barbarians are caught between civilized and uncivilized ways of living. They want a share in the good things of civilized living. They may trade peacefully to get such things. Yet they are just as likely to take what they want by force—if they can.

- Review the physical features of Sumer. Did Sumer have many natural defenses?

- Why would it have been especially easy for the barbarians to attack Sumerian cities during the years we have described?

- How might barbarians become civilized?

The Idea of Civilization Spreads to Other River Valleys

We have looked at some geographic and political changes in Sumer during the third millennium B.C. All of these things caused Sumerian culture to grow weak and finally to die out. By the time it did die out, civilization itself was well under way. Remember that a culture of a people, their government, their laws, and their way of life may die out. But the idea of civilization with its cities, surplus of goods, and division of labor did not die out. In fact, civilization was spreading.

- Review the changes and problems that weakened Sumerian culture.

- Why is it possible to say that Sumerian culture was growing weak, but civilization was healthy?

About 3100 B.C., in the valley of the Nile River, the Egyptians began to build the second oldest civilization. By 2500 B.C., people living in the valley of the Indus River had also built a civilization. All three of these civilizations—the Sumerian, the Egyptian, and the Indus River—began *independently*. That means that each began separately and apart from the others.

Yet ideas spread easily. They spread easily even in ancient times. Probably the idea of civilization was spread through trade and travel. Wherever the idea was spread, people learned that it was possible to settle down in one place, build cities, and find a better way of life.

Once the Egyptian and Indus River Valley civilizations were under way, their people came in touch with each other. They learned ideas and skills from each other and from the Sumerians. Each civilization could borrow these new ideas and skills. Each civilization, in turn, could act as a center from which the idea of civilization could spread.

● How would trade and travel help to spread civilization?

War was another way in which civilization was spread from the dying Sumerian culture. Let us learn some of the ways in which war spread civilization throughout the Middle East.

A Sumerian king leading his troops into battle. The soldiers are marching over the dead bodies of their enemy.

Sargon the Mighty

The land of Akkad (ak' ad) lay north of Sumer. The Akkadians (ə kā' dē ənz) had lived side by side with the Sumerians for a long time. They had been herdsmen. Over the years the Akkadians copied many civilized ways of doing things. After a time their chiefs began to copy the Sumerian way of producing food. They began to turn away from herding as a way of life. Then they began to organize the work of irrigation and farming in Akkad.

Sargon was one of these chiefs. He organized the Akkadians into a strong fighting force. He became a military king. This is how he described himself: "Sargon the mighty, King of Akkad, am I." He was indeed mighty. About 2300 B.C., Sargon moved his army south. One by one he conquered the cities of Sumer. For the first time Sumer fell under foreign rule. Sargon began to call himself King of Sumer and Akkad.

Sargon's rule did not change the lives of the average Sumerian very much. The work of irrigating and producing food still had to go on as before. Of course, even more people had to be fed and supported. The city-state kings were now forced to pay money and goods to Sargon, the conqueror.

The Blending of Cultures

Everyday life in Akkad and Sumer did not change all at once. Gradually, however, Sargon's reign brought important changes. One big change was in language. The language of the Akkadians became the language used for everyday matters. The Sumerian language was used only for religious purposes. The Akkadians took over the cuneiform writing of the Sumerians. They used it to put their own language into written form. They used the Sumerian cuneiform marks to stand for the sounds in their own language. There were also changes in religion. The Akkadians began to worship Sumerian gods. There was a general *blending together of the two cultures.*

- Two cultures gradually became one under Sargon. Explain what had happened to the Akkadians in the process.

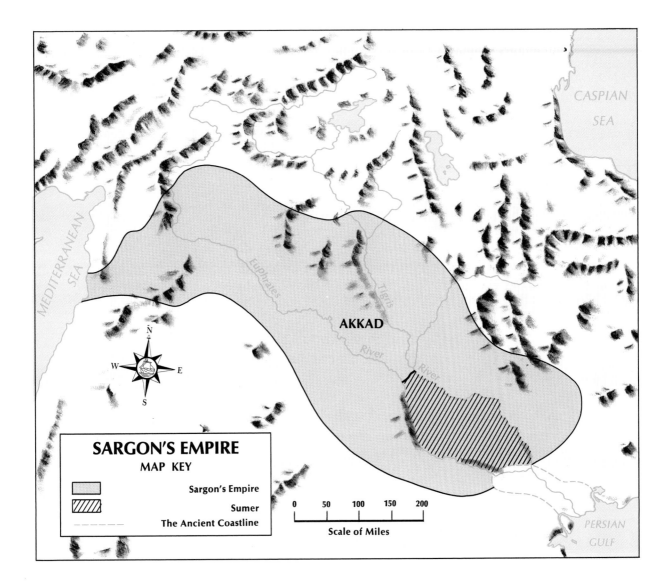

SARGON'S EMPIRE
MAP KEY

Sargon's Empire
Sumer
The Ancient Coastline

0   50   100   150   200

Scale of Miles

Sargon united all the Sumerian city-states and Akkad into an empire. Then he added other lands to his empire until he controlled all of Mesopotamia. The map above shows how large his empire became. He must have made raids with his army over long distances. He may even have reached the coasts of the Black Sea and the Mediterranean.

The river valley civilization was about to become part of a much larger area. This larger area included land that was well watered by rain. On such land irrigation was not needed for the growing of crops. Civilization was about to spread from the irrigated river valleys to rain-watered land.

Many scholars believe that this is
a bronze head of King Sargon.

The Fall of Sargon's Empire

Sargon did not have an easy time ruling his large empire. He set a pattern of rule that later rulers adopted. This pattern of rule continued throughout much of the history of the Middle East. Sargon's armies did not settle down with the people they conquered. Instead, they simply made these people give them food or other goods.

The Sumerians did not like this treatment. Sumerian city-states often tried to revolt. Herders and small farmers who had to work for the Akkadians tried to revolt, too. They wanted a bigger share in the good things civilization brought. Barbarians often waited until a revolt broke out. They knew that would be a good time to attack.

Sargon's empire was too large for him to control easily. In his lifetime, he fought over 30 wars trying to keep his empire in one piece. Sargon's grandson, in his turn, pushed the boundaries of the empire even farther away from Mesopotamia. When he died, however, barbarians overran the land. The empire fell.

● What problems did Sargon face from within his empire? From outside his empire?

Hammurabi and the Triumph of Babylon

After the fall of Sargon's empire, events in Mesopotamia did not change a great deal. There continued to be many wars, and there was much confusion. New barbarians attacked civilization and created empires. They became civilized. Then, in time, they, too, were attacked by other barbarians.

In the eighteenth century B.C., a man named Hammurabi (hä′ mü ̄rä′ bē) became king of the city-state of Babylon. He went far beyond the boundaries of Babylon to Mesopotamia. There he became the ruler of a great new empire. He took over control of the Sumerian-Akkadian culture. The map on page 116 shows how large his empire became.

Once again there was a blending of cultures. The Babylonians took over the combined Sumerian-Akkadian culture. They took over its writing, its customs, and its ways of doing things.

They adopted the same Sumerian gods that the Akkadians had worshipped. However, they gave Babylonian names to these gods.

Hammurabi was a great leader and a wise man. He sent out his soldiers to live among the people in his empire. He appointed officials to rule for him throughout the empire. He appointed tax collectors. He drew up a code of laws. Hammurabi's laws were fair and just laws. Hammurabi appointed royal judges to see that his laws were carried out.

● Why are laws necessary in a civilization? Why would Hammurabi's laws be so very important?

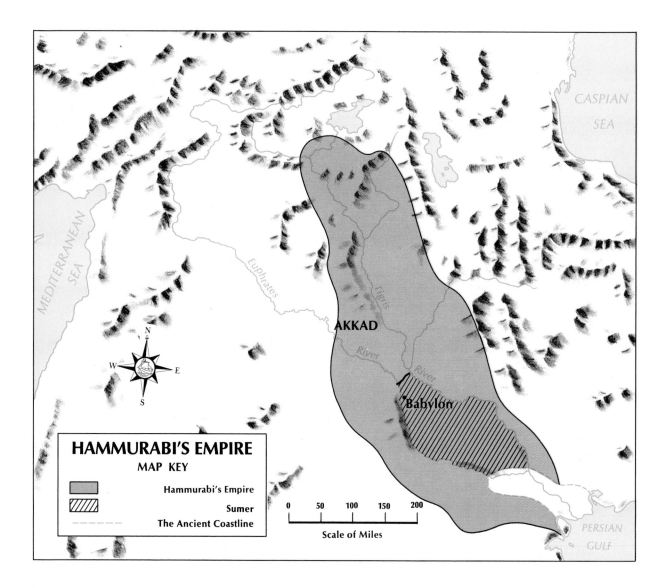

Hammurabi, king of Babylon, stands before the sun god. This sculpture appears at the top of a long stone slab which contains Hammurabi's law code written in cuneiform.

By this time the original Sumerian culture was almost forgotten. It survived under new names and in new forms. But no one remembered where the culture had come from. For the next 12 centuries, Babylon was the great power. Middle Eastern history—with all its ups and downs—had become Babylonian history. This idea of the rise and fall of civilization is one that we will meet often in the course of *The Human Adventure*.

- What are some possible causes of the rise and fall of civilization? You will find several clues in the chapter you have just read.

- Why and how might barbarians be able to defeat civilized people?

- Civilization, itself, has never died out, and it has never been forgotten. Try to explain why.

Written records are important clues to archaeologists in their study of ancient civilizations. The illustration above shows an example of Egyptian picture writing, called hieroglyphics. Below is an example of picture writing from the Indus Valley.

chapter 7

The Spread of Civilization

River Valley Civilizations

For about 1,500 years, civilization was found only in river valleys. The map on page 120 shows the three earliest civilizations. Note the locations of the Indus Valley, the Tigris-Euphrates Valley, and the Nile Valley.

● Do you think that the people on the Indus and on the Nile may have learned about civilization from the Sumerians? Why? How?

● Review the reasons why civilization was possible in such great river valleys.

We have read a great deal about the exciting discovery of Sumer and the things that archaeologists have been able to learn about the Sumerians. As we move on in *The Human Adventure*, we will not study so deeply the ancient civilizations of the Nile and Indus Valleys. We will read only briefly about these interesting peoples.

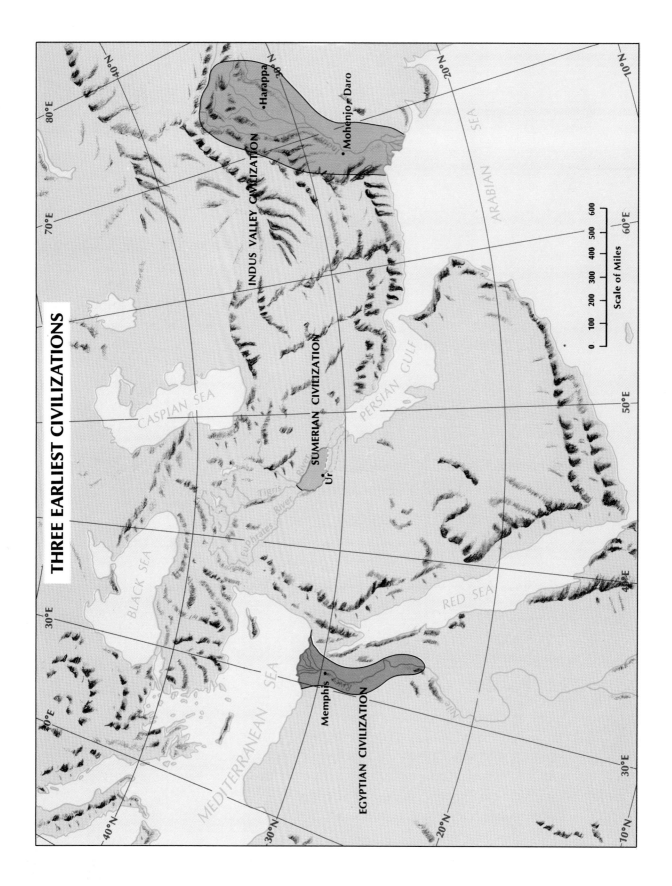

THREE EARLIEST CIVILIZATIONS

INDUS VALLEY CIVILIZATION

Harappa

Mohenjo-Daro

Indus River

ARABIAN SEA

SUMERIAN CIVILIZATION

Ur

Tigris River

Euphrates River

PERSIAN GULF

CASPIAN SEA

BLACK SEA

MEDITERRANEAN SEA

EGYPTIAN CIVILIZATION

Memphis

Nile River

RED SEA

Scale of Miles

0 100 200 300 400 500 600

Egypt: The Nile Valley Civilization

Until a few years ago people thought that civilization first appeared in Egypt. Then the civilization of Sumer was discovered. Now scholars believe that Egypt was the second, not the first, civilization.

★ What is the land of Egypt called today?

Let us see what the land of Egypt was like. The Nile River flows northward out of central Africa for 4,000 miles. For the last 600 of these miles, the river cuts through the land that was Ancient Egypt. From the air, the Nile River Valley looks like a thin, green ribbon on a brown paper package. In most places the valley is 10 to 20 miles wide. In a few places it is as narrow as two or three miles.

Like the Sumerians, the ancient Egyptians had to learn to control their physical environment. However, the physical environment of the Egyptians was different from that of the Sumerians. The Egyptians had to find different ways of controlling it.

The Sumerians built their civilization along two rivers. The Egyptians built their civilization along one river. The Nile was easier to control than the Tigris and Euphrates. It was not as violent. Every summer the Nile gently overflowed its banks. As it

Egyptians used the yearly flooding of the Nile to help build their civilization.

did so, it covered the land with muddy water. The Egyptians found their own way to use the flood water and irrigate the land.

The Egyptians dug **catchment basins**. These were places that had been dug out to hold the flood waters. The Egyptians invented a machine to raise water from the river into the catchment basins. This machine was called a **shadoof** (shä düf'). After the floods, the land began to dry out. Then the water held in the catchment basins could be let out into the fields. In Egypt, irrigation took less time and work than in Sumer. Like the Sumerians, however, the Egyptians learned to work together to develop a surplus of food.

By working together, the Egyptians were able to build a mighty civilization. We know that they developed many skills. They had a system of writing and figured out a way of making a kind of paper. They learned how to build well with stone. Their artists made beautiful pottery and carved statues from stone. We have also been able to learn a great deal about their religion and their government. The Egyptian civilization lasted longer than the Sumerian civilization, and it was never forgotten.

A shadoof works on the same idea as a see-saw. One end of the pole is weighted. The man pulls down on the rope at the other end of the pole to lower the bucket into the water. When he releases the bucket, the weights lift it back to the level of the catchment basin.

Fish appear often in Egyptian art because the Nile River was so important to Egyptian life. This small fish is made of colored glass.

Why did Egyptian civilization last much longer than Sumer? Perhaps the most important reason was that Egypt was easy to defend. The map on page 120 will help you to understand why. As you look at the map, remember that the civilization was located along the narrow valley of the Nile and at the mouths of the Nile.

- What natural defenses did Egypt have? If barbarians wanted to attack Egypt how could they do it? What difficulties would they face?

- How would the Nile help to unite the people? How would it help the ruler to control the people?

- What is the name of the landform at the mouths of the Nile?

Another reason for the long life of Egyptian civilization was its strong government. From early times the Egyptians had strong rulers. These rulers were called **pharaohs** (fãr′ōz).

Huge pyramids were built as tombs for pharaohs. Egyptians believed that a pharaoh's soul would live forever. Therefore, they filled the tombs with everything he would need in the next world. The model figures below were found in a tomb. They are servants carrying supplies for the pharaoh.

Egyptian craftsmen had great skill.
The duck vase and painted ointment jars
are beautiful examples of their work.

Egyptians took time out for play. Shown here is a game called "hounds and jackals." The five playing pieces with ears pointed up are the jackals. The five with ears down are the hounds. Knucklebones were used as dice to decide how the pieces were moved around the board.

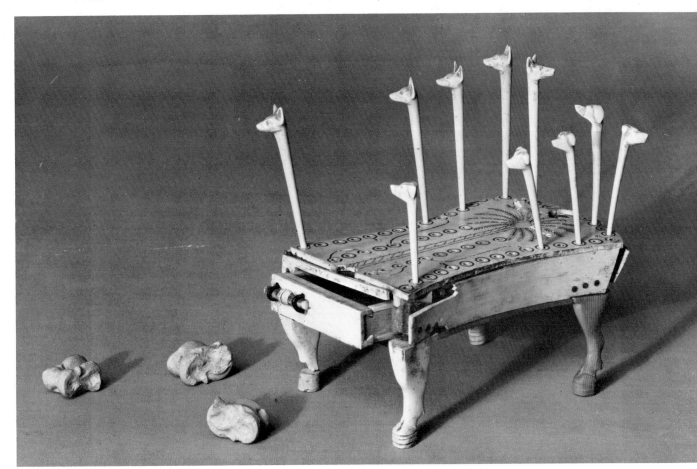

Because Egyptian civilization was never buried or forgotten, historians have been writing about it since early times. Many of its buildings remain standing. Thousands of artifacts have been found. You remember that in the study of Sumer, archaeologists used many different clues to understand the way of life of the Sumerians. This is also true in the study of Egypt. Archaeologists, today, use the writings of historians as one way of learning about ancient civilization in Egypt. Just as in the study of Sumer, they also use many artifacts to understand Egyptian culture. Like the Sumerians, the Egyptians left written records of their own. Their system of writing was different from the Sumerian cuneiform. However, when archaeologists learned to read Egyptian writing, it gave them still another clue in their study of Egypt's ancient civilization. Like the study of Sumer, the study of Egypt is still going on. Archaeologists continue to find artifacts and written records. These discoveries add to our knowledge of this ancient river valley civilization.

Like women today, Egyptian women believed that jewelry made them more beautiful. This collar necklace was delicately made from gold and semiprecious stones.

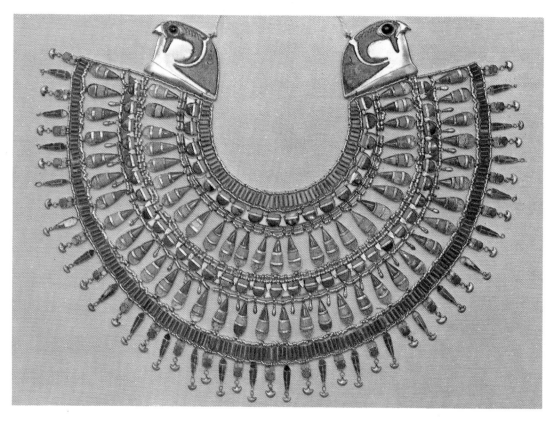

The figures of this powerful Egyptian pharaoh and his queen were carved from slate.

Museum of Fine Arts, Boston

Statue of an
Indus Valley man

The Civilization of the Indus Valley

There was one other early river valley civilization. Cities grew up more than a thousand miles east of Sumer. These cities were on the Indus River. When archaeologists began to dig in this area, they found two great cities. One was called Harappa (hə rap′ ə). Harappa was in the north. The other was Mohenjo-Daro (mō hen′ jō där′ ō). Mohenjo-Daro was 400 miles southwest of Harappa. The sites of Harappa and Mohenjo-Daro are in an area which today is called West Pakistan. Locate the Indus Valley civilization on the map on page 120.

We have already seen how civilization arose in Sumer and Egypt. The Indus River people did just about the same things the Sumerians and Egyptians did. They irrigated the land by using the waters of the Indus River. They created a surplus of food. Some men did special jobs. They built cities.

What were these cities like? They had wide streets, laid out in squares. Tall houses of baked brick looked out on the streets. The people who lived there had knowledge of plumbing. They had bathrooms in their houses and drain pipes to carry away waste.

We know something about the religion of these people of long ago. They worshipped many gods. The priests learned to read and write. Their script is shown on many seals. In the ruins of the cities, children's toys have been found. So have many fine pots. We know, too, that the people were good at working in gold, silver, copper, and lead. The craftsmen of Harappa and Mohenjo-Daro made beautiful small statues.

Like Sumer, but unlike Egypt, the Indus civilization was forgotten for thousands of years. The great cities died. Their ruins were buried under mud and sand. They were not found again until about 50 years ago.

Why did the cities die? Why was all trace of them lost? We cannot be sure, but scholars have made some guesses. Perhaps the people used up the soil around the cities. Perhaps the river changed its course. Perhaps, too, there were terrible floods. Or the climate may have changed. Another explanation might be that some illness killed off the people.

A child of the Indus Valley once played with this animal-drawn clay cart. A great many of these toys have been found. As a result, many scholars believe that they were made to be used for trade with other ancient peoples.

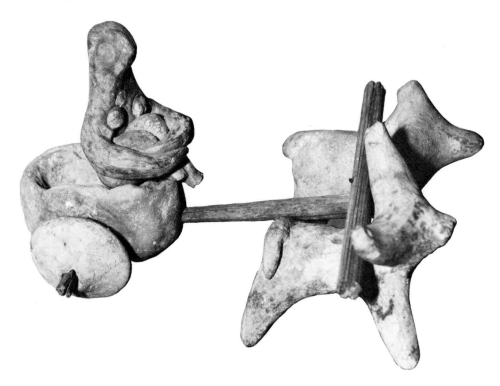

This clay statue is one of many models of bulls found in the Indus Valley. The figure of the bull may have had religious importance for the people of this civilization.

Below are the ruins of Mohenjo-Daro. Archaeologists believe that this city was carefully planned before it was built. It was laid out in square blocks, with main streets and smaller alleys. The drainage ditch, opposite, was built along the sides of the houses.

This clay female figure, wearing a headdress and other ornaments, may represent a goddess.

A pottery bowl from the Indus Valley

We know, too, that an invasion happened around 1500 B.C. About that time barbarians came across the northwest mountains. They called themselves Aryans (ãr' i ənz). They conquered all northern India. We do not know if they brought the Indus civilization to a bloody end. The cities of Harappa and Mohenjo-Daro may have been ruined before the Aryans came. The Aryans did not take over or rebuild these cities. So the Indus civilization faded from human memory.

Archaeologists continue to explore in the Indus Valley to learn as much as possible about this early civilization. They work in the same way that archaeologists do in the study of Egypt and Sumer. They guess what they can about the Indus Valley people by carefully studying the buildings and the artifacts they find. Like the Sumerians and the Egyptians, the Indus Valley people developed a system of writing. Archaeologists have found written records, but they have one great problem. They have not been able to understand these records. They have not yet found a key to this writing. This problem has made the study of the Indus Valley civilization very difficult.

- Sumer's civilization was conquered and taken over by other people. What civilizations then followed in Mesopotamia?

- How important are written records to archaeologists in their study of ancient peoples? What difference will it make in the study of the Indus Valley people if archaeologists learn to read their writing?

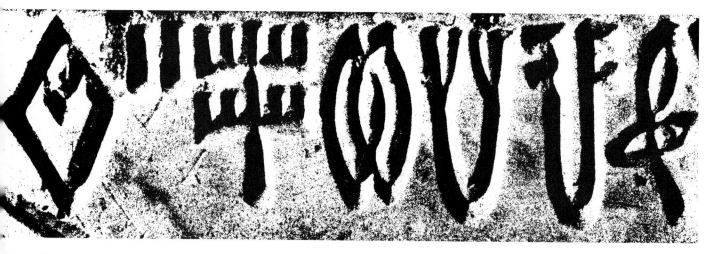

Civilization Spreads to Rain-Watered Lands

About 4,000 years ago, it seemed that civilization was possible only in river valleys. Such valleys were flooded once a year. Men learned to use the floods for irrigation by digging canals or catchment basins. Irrigation made it possible to produce surplus food. With a surplus of food, came division of labor and the growth of cities. As men settled down, they developed new areas of knowledge and new forms of government. Each early society which developed a civilization went through this order of change.

Could civilization develop in other environments? We know that men had been growing crops long before they found out about irrigation. Most early agriculture had been found in **rain-watered** lands. These are lands that have enough regular rainfall to grow crops without the use of irrigation. Rain-watered agriculture, like irrigated agriculture, could produce a surplus which is necessary for civilization to develop.

Civilization began in irrigated river valleys. It was later in coming to rain-watered lands and slower to develop there. Why do you think this happened? The following questions will help you to answer.

- Would it be easier for men to grow food on irrigated land or on land watered by rainfall? Explain.

- On which type of land would men be more likely to work together in large numbers to produce a surplus? Explain.

- Where would a small group be more likely to gain control of the surplus? Why?

- How would control of the surplus by a small group influence the rise of civilization?

We know that about 2000 B.C. civilization did begin to spread from the river valleys of Mesopotamia to rain-watered lands. By this time, civilization was also spreading out from its other centers—Egypt and the Indus River Valley. Civilization was on the move.

How did this happen? We have already seen many of the ways that civilization was spread. Warfare spread civilization.

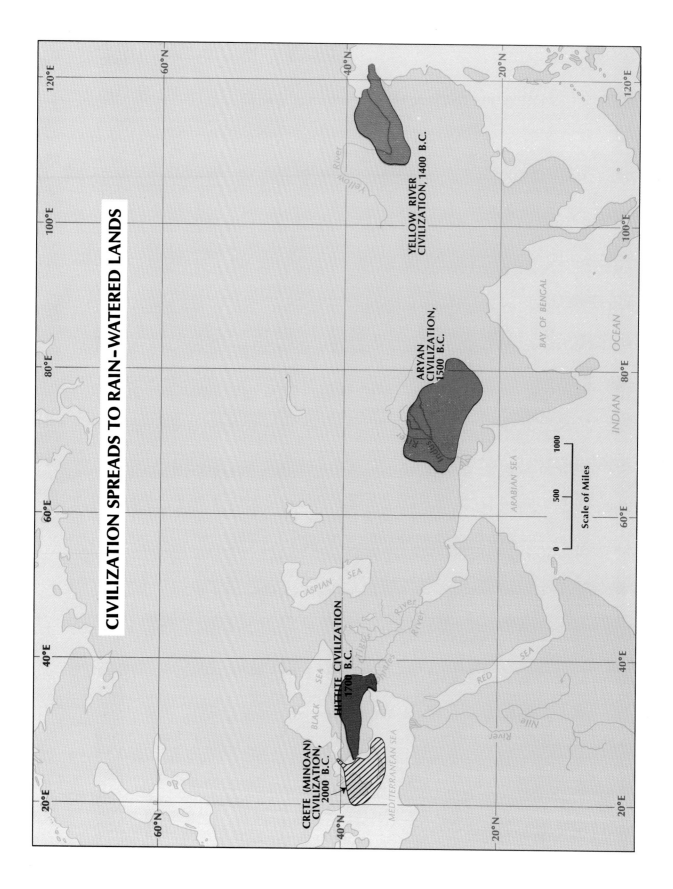

CIVILIZATION SPREADS TO RAIN-WATERED LANDS

YELLOW RIVER CIVILIZATION, 1400 B.C.

ARYAN CIVILIZATION, 1500 B.C.

HITTITE CIVILIZATION 1700 B.C.

CRETE (MINOAN) CIVILIZATION, 2000 B.C.

Scale of Miles

0   500   1000

Trade and travel spread civilization. Barbarians, living on the edges of civilization, copied civilized ways of doing things. In doing so they became civilized themselves.

In the next section of this chapter, we are going to read about the effect of warfare on the development of civilization in rain-watered lands. If a strong ruler was able to take the surplus food grown by farmers, he could then use it to feed other workers. These workers could help to build cities and do many other jobs for the ruler. The surplus could also be used to support a strong army.

That is what happened. After about 2000 B.C., rulers and conquerors used their armies to take over peoples in rain-watered lands. The farmers were often forced to give up their surplus. Then the rulers used the surplus in any way they wished. The farmers did most of the work. The rulers got most of the benefits of that work. They were able to support their own groups of specialists. They built up royal households and cities around these specialists. Through the use of military force, these rulers were building new civilizations. All the changes first seen in the river valleys of Sumer now appeared in Asia Minor and on the shores of the Mediterranean.

The map on the opposite page shows the spread of civilization to rain-watered lands. Make sure you can identify the locations of the older river valley civilizations. Notice the new rain-watered civilization in Crete, developed by the Minoans (mi nō′ ənz) around 2000 B.C., and the one in Asia Minor, developed by the Hittites (hit′ īts) around 1700 B.C. The Aryan invasion of northern India, which brought great change to the Indus Valley, took place around 1500 B.C. Find the new river valley and rain-watered civilization on the Yellow River in northern China, which developed around 1400 B.C.

● Some people think that farmers had a better life before civilization came to them. What do you think?

A New Way of Fighting: The War Chariot

Every so often new weapons and new ways of fighting appear. When they appear, they are likely to bring great change. A new way of fighting appeared about 1700 B.C. It came with barbarian invaders, and it upset the civilized parts of the world.

In fighting their wars the Sumerian armies used four-wheeled carts drawn by donkeys. The barbarians borrowed this idea and improved on it. They made a small, two-wheeled battle cart called a **chariot**. With the chariot came a new way of fighting. The chariot was pulled by horses instead of donkeys. It was much better than the clumsy Sumerian carts. It could be turned quickly and easily. The horses could pull chariots swiftly across the battlefields.

Two men, charioteers, rode in each chariot. One man drove the horses. The other used a small, powerful bow to shoot arrows at the enemy. Foot soldiers could not stand up under chariot attacks. They were forced to scatter. While the foot soldiers were still scattered and confused, the charioteers joined together again. Once more the chariots would rush across the plains. This time it would be a mass attack. The charioteers killed everyone in their path.

There was only one time when the men on foot could defeat the charioteers. That was when the charioteers were also on foot. This happened when they were camped and their horses were unharnessed. However, they soon found a way to protect themselves in open country. When they set up camp, they built special forts of earth and wood. From the forts they could fight almost as well as they could fight from the chariots.

New Empires Come into Being

The charioteers attacked wherever they pleased. No power could stop them. They destroyed the outer edges of civilization first. Then they started to destroy the river valley civilizations. Barbarians won control over Egypt about 1700 B.C. Other barbarians invaded the valley of the Indus River. That civilization was at an end by 1500 B.C. Barbarians also overran all of Mesopotamia, the birthplace of civilization. Everywhere, they won by force of military strength.

Yet civilization grew again. The old pattern repeated itself. After the barbarians conquered a land, they settled down and became civilized. How did this happen? First, the barbarian kings divided the land among their followers. These followers became rulers. As rulers, they forced the people of the cities and villages to work for them. The rulers took what they wanted from what the people produced. Civilization began again with new rulers.

● In what ways had the barbarians copied the ideas and ways of civilization?

Out of this confusion three great empires developed. In the valley of the Nile, the Egyptians overthrew their foreign rulers.

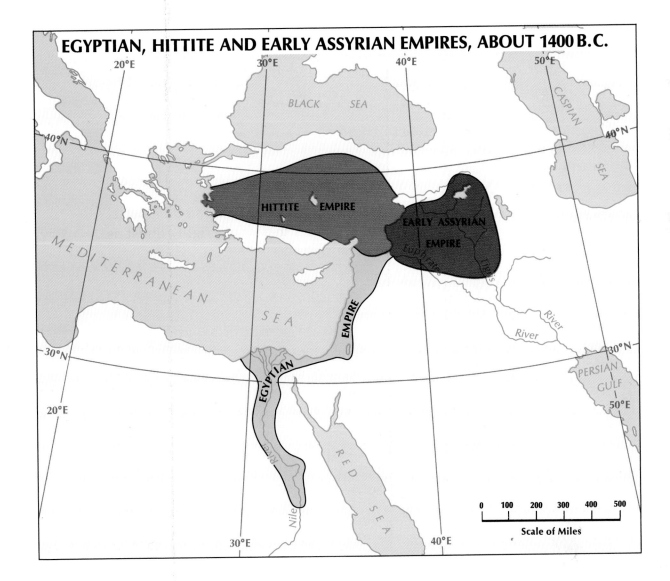

EGYPTIAN, HITTITE AND EARLY ASSYRIAN EMPIRES, ABOUT 1400 B.C.

The Egyptians then began to build an empire. They pushed their power and control southward along the Nile into central Africa. They pushed northeast out of the river valley itself. Soon they controlled the land east of the Mediterranean Sea. At about the same time, people called the Hittites took over all the land between the Mediterranean and the Black Seas. They, too, built a mighty empire. The third great empire was built by the Assyrians (ə sir′ ē ənz). They came to power a bit later. They ruled the entire area of northern Mesopotamia. Locate these three empires on the map on page 137.

Iron Weapons and Another Wave of Barbarians

Shortly after 1500 B.C., civilization was found in all parts of the Middle East. The early civilized centers of Mesopotamia and Egypt grew much larger. The land of these two ancient centers began to border on the newly civilized areas. The result was a larger, more united center of civilization. This does not mean that all the different cultures became one. They did not. It does mean that the center of civilization had become large enough to include *all* the area we call the Middle East.

Then trouble started all over again. Beginning about 1200 B.C., the ancient world was once more swept by barbarian attacks. The three-way division of power between the Hittites, the Assyrians, and the Egyptians was upset. The Hittite empire was almost completely destroyed. The Assyrian and Egyptian empires grew weak.

Again the barbarians gained their victories through new weapons. Chariots had once been the new and superior weapons. Now they were only second best. They were being used by civilized men. The barbarians had begun to use *iron*. Iron was cheap, and large armies could easily be equipped with iron weapons. With these weapons, barbarians could defeat the civilized charioteers.

This time the barbarians borrowed a skill from civilization. It was the skill of metalworking. They used this skill the way earlier barbarians had used a borrowed idea. With it they conquered civilized people. In time, these barbarians settled down and became civilized, too.

▶ What idea had earlier barbarians borrowed from civilization?

At first the Assyrians were weakened by the barbarian attacks. Then they recovered and became strong. Starting about 1100 B.C., the Assyrians became the strongest power in the Middle East. The Assyrians were known for their brutal ways. They were powerful, and they were very cruel. The Assyrians built an empire that included nearly all of the Middle East.

An Assyrian archer and his attendant. How do we know from this carved relief that the Assyrians were skilled in metalworking?

Archery and horseback riding were important skills in sport, as well as in war. Here, an Assyrian king takes aim during a lion hunt.

The people who had to live under Assyrian rule were not happy. There were many revolts from within the Assyrian empire. At the same time the Assyrians were faced with barbarian attacks from outside the empire. This combination proved to be too much for them. They could not handle troubles from both inside and outside the empire. Besides, the barbarians had learned to use still newer methods of fighting. Thus the pattern repeated itself.

The attacking barbarians were excellent horsemen. They could shoot arrows and hit a target while galloping at top speed. A horse could move around more easily on a battlefield than a bulky chariot. A single rider could also move more quickly than two men in a chariot. With this skill the barbarians were able to destroy the capital city of the Assyrians. Assyrian power crumbled. Another empire had risen and fallen.

The Last Great Empire of the Ancient Middle East: The Persians

After the power of the Assyrians had been destroyed, still another people gained strength. Soon they were in control of the Middle East. These people were the Persians. The Persians, in turn, became civilized. They built the last great empire of the ancient Middle East. The Persians did what the Assyrians had tried to do. They succeeded in uniting the whole Middle East under one power. By then it was 525 B.C.

Civilization had come a long way in 3,000 years. From its beginning in Sumer, it had spread far and wide. By the sixth century B.C., a large part of the world was civilized. This civilized area was made up of many cultures. In time, civilization was to spread to still other areas of the world.

The great palace of the Persian kings was built in the city of Persepolis. This stone animal was found among the city's ruins.

conclusion

The Ebb and Flow of Civilization

Scholars often speak of the rise and fall of civilization. Between 3500 and 500 B.C. there were many rises and falls. Yet civilization itself never disappeared. Perhaps it is better to say that civilization **ebbs and flows**. It is like a tide in the ocean. The tide rises, or flows, to cover the sands of the shore. Then it falls, or ebbs, leaving the sands dry. Then the tide flows again. Then ebbs.

Like the ocean, civilization goes up and down. Sometimes civilization is strong. Sometimes it is weak.

As the Human Adventure continued, civilization spread further and further from its beginnings in Mesopotamia. By 500 B.C., civilization was found in the Middle East, northern India, the eastern Mediterranean, and northern China. From these areas, it spread to other parts of the world.

As civilization spreads, it changes to suit different cultures.

Thousands of years have passed since the Sumerians built their civilization. Their culture has disappeared, but civilization still exists today in "the land between two rivers."

We have already said that for civilization to develop in an area, three things must be true. The people must have a surplus of food, division of labor, and cities. However, this does not mean that each civilization developed in exactly the same way. Each group of people has a culture of its own. The people of different civilizations may borrow ideas from one another. Yet, at the same time, each civilization has its own way of life.

We have seen that when civilization developed in Sumer, it brought many important changes to the people. As civilization spread, it carried changes to larger and larger areas of the world. The following questions will help you to review some of the important ideas we have learned about civilization. They will help you to remember what kinds of changes civilization may bring to a society.

▶ Look at the "Time Line of Ancient Civilization." It will help you to review the ebb and flow of civilization over the period we have studied.

▶ What do we mean by *civilization*? What do we mean by *barbarians*? What signs would you look for in a society to find out if it was civilized or not?

● The growth of civilization brings changes in the economic life of a society. What do the following *economic* terms have to do with the growth of civilization?

    surplus production
    capital or savings
    division of labor, or specialization
    managers
    workers
    trade
    money

● How does civilization bring about different groups of people in a society? Are all these groups equal in wealth? In the kind of work they do? In the power they hold?

● Does civilization help to increase men's *knowledge*? Does it help to bring *better ways of doing things*? Explain and give examples.

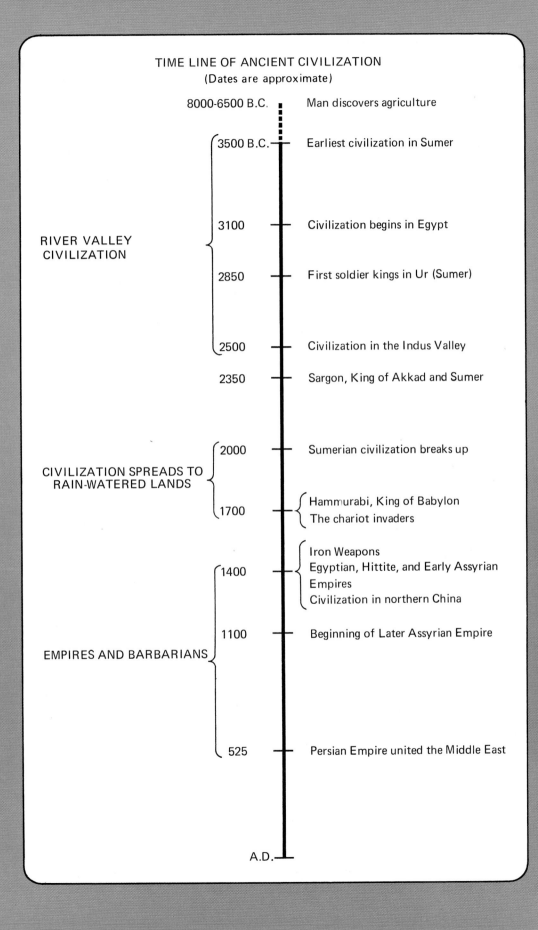

TIME LINE OF ANCIENT CIVILIZATION
(Dates are approximate)

8000-6500 B.C. — Man discovers agriculture

3500 B.C. — Earliest civilization in Sumer

3100 — Civilization begins in Egypt

2850 — First soldier kings in Ur (Sumer)

2500 — Civilization in the Indus Valley

2350 — Sargon, King of Akkad and Sumer

2000 — Sumerian civilization breaks up

1700 — Hammurabi, King of Babylon
The chariot invaders

1400 — Iron Weapons
Egyptian, Hittite, and Early Assyrian Empires
Civilization in northern China

1100 — Beginning of Later Assyrian Empire

525 — Persian Empire united the Middle East

A.D. —

RIVER VALLEY CIVILIZATION

CIVILIZATION SPREADS TO RAIN-WATERED LANDS

EMPIRES AND BARBARIANS

- The growth of civilization brings changes to the *government* of a society. The following words all have to do with government. Can you explain why? Can you think of any ways in which the growth of civilization would change the government of a society?

rulers	armies
officials	wars
laws	empires
taxes	

- Does civilization go with *better control over man's environment*? Explain and give examples. Does civilization sometimes *harm the environment*? How?

- List some of the possible reasons for the ebb (fall or weakening) of civilization.

- How may *new ways of war* bring changes in civilization and empires? Give some examples.

- Look again at the chart on page 60, which lists important questions to ask about a culture. What do we mean by *culture*? Which questions are important in helping to see the differences between one culture and another? Which would help you to tell whether or not a culture was civilized?

One of the things that is special about man is that he can learn from the past. Because he can think, he is not always satisfied with doing things in the same way. He asks questions. He uses old ideas but develops new ideas as well. Man learned to control his environment by using his mind. This made possible the beginning of civilization. Civilization, in turn, gave man more time to think.

Ideas are among the most important parts of a culture. Man has ideas about god and about the meaning of life. He has ideas about right and wrong. Man's ideas have a great influence on his actions and the way he lives. We have seen how the Sumerians' ideas about the meaning of life influenced their whole culture. The Sumerians lived a very long time ago. Their ideas may be hard for us to grasp. However, these ideas were very important to the Sumerians. They helped to control or guide the Sumerian way of life.

In the next part of *The Human Adventure*, we shall study the controlling ideas of four other cultures. These cultures were developing during the period we have been studying. Certain great ideas about religion and philosophy were set down about the sixth century B.C. These ideas are the keys to understanding four cultures of that time: the cultures of the Chinese, the Indians, the Hebrews, and the Greeks. They are also the keys to understanding many cultures in our world of today.

Confucius, a great teacher, lived in the sixth century B.C. He had an important effect on the controlling ideas of Chinese culture.

GLOSSARY

Some words have many meanings. This list gives only the meanings of words as they are used in this book. To find other meanings of these words, look them up in a dictionary.

agriculture: farming; art of cultivating the soil, producing crops, and raising livestock.

Akkad: home of the Akkadians, who first attacked and conquered Sumer.

A.D.: abbreviation of the Latin words *anno Domini*, meaning in the year of our Lord; used to date events that took place after the birth of Jesus Christ.

archaeologist: scientist who studies ancient ruins and artifacts in order to learn about the past.

archaeology: the scientific study of the past by digging up and studying the objects that ancient peoples made and used. (See history.)

artifact: a man-made object, such as a tool, a weapon, a statue, or an ornament.

Aryans: barbarian invaders who conquered northern India about 1500 B.C.

assembly: a number of persons gathered together for political purposes.

Assyrians: people who built an empire in the Middle East after the time of the Sumerians.

axis: the imaginary line that runs through the center of the earth and connects the poles.

Babylonia: part of Mesopotamia after the time of Sumer; now part of Iraq.

barbarians: people who live on the edges of civilization and want a share in the good things of civilized living.

barter: a simple form of trading through the exchange of goods.

B.C.: abbreviation of before Christ; used to date events that took place in the years before the birth of Jesus Christ.

blending: a coming together and mixing of two or more ideas to produce something new.

calendar: the way men arrange time into days, weeks, months, and years. The calendar we use today uses the year Jesus Christ was born as a starting point.

capital: surplus goods used as savings to improve the production of goods. Goods used to produce other goods are called *capital goods*. We call machinery, irrigation canals, tools, factories, capital goods.

captivity: the state of being made or held a prisoner.

catchment basin: hole dug by men to catch and hold flood water.

century: 100 years.

chariot: two-wheeled horse-drawn battle car.

city-state: a city plus the land around it that has its own independent government.

civilization: a condition of life in which a people have a surplus of goods, a division of labor, and cities.

civilized: description given to a people who have a surplus of goods, a division of labor, and cities.

climate: average weather conditions over a period of years.

craft: an art, a trade, or an occupation that requires special skill.

culture: the traditions and customs of a people; way of life.

cuneiform: wedge-shaped marks; writing invented by the Sumerians.

cylinder seal: a picture or design carved on a piece of stone or pottery that could be rolled across a clay tablet; used by ancient peoples to sign their names.

decade: 10 years.

degrees of latitude: a system for measuring distance north and south of the equator. (See parallels of latitude.)

degrees of longitude: a system of measuring distance east and west of the prime meridian. (See meridans and prime meridian.)

distribute: to divide and give out in shares.

division of labor: a separation of workers into different jobs so that more and better goods can be produced. Another name for this is *specialization*.

ebb and flow of civilization: a process in man's history in which one culture declines and falls, and is followed in time by the rise of another. The idea of civilization, however, continues and is passed from one culture to another.

economic life: the way people make and obtain goods. It includes their system of labor, manufacture, and trade.

economics: the scientific study of how goods and services are produced, distributed, and used.

edubba: the Sumerian word for school.

education: the process of learning how to live in one's society, and acquiring knowledge and developing the power to reason and judge.

Egyptians: people who built an ancient civilization in the Nile River Valley.

empire: the area conquered and controlled by a single supreme power.

Enkidu: the friend and companion of Gilgamesh.

Enlil: Sumerian god of the air who separated heaven and earth.

equator: an imaginary line drawn around the earth at an equal distance from the north and south poles. It divides the earth into northern and southern hemispheres. It is zero degrees of latitude.

family: the basic social group. It may be made up of parents and their children. The extended family might include grandparents, aunts, uncles, cousins, certain in-laws.

flood plain: plain which borders on a river and is made of soil deposited by floods.

force of nature: a physical force that man cannot control, such as the sun, moon, rain, thunder, etc.

geography: the study of the earth, including such things as climate, soil, relief, vegetation, population; also includes the study of man's use of the land.

Gilgamesh: a Sumerian hero whose mighty deeds are told in the oldest poem in history, *The Epic of Gilgamesh*.

grid: made by the criss-crossing of lines which run north-south and east-west on a map.

grid lines: the lines on a grid. Grid lines divide a map into sections or squares.

grid map: a map with grid lines on it.

government: the men who rule a society.

Hammurabi: Babylonian king.

Harappa: one of the two known cities of the Indus River Valley civilization.

hemisphere: a half of the earth's surface. The earth is divided into northern and southern hemispheres by the equator.

Herodotus: a great historian of the ancient world. He was a Greek.

history: the study of the past through written records. (See archaeology.)

Hittites: people who built an empire in the Middle East long after the time of the Sumerians.

Humbaba: the evil giant destroyed by Gilgamesh.

Indus: a river valley in northern India where an early civilization developed. Today the region is part of Pakistan.

Iran: modern name for Persia.

Iraq: modern name for Mesopotamia.

irrigation: method of supplying the land with water by artificial means, such as ditches, channels, canals.

knowledge: body of truths or facts gathered by men in the course of time.

latitude: a distance in degrees north and south of the equator.

law: rule of conduct set up and enforced by the authority, legislation, or custom of a community. Sometimes "the law" is used to mean all the rules of a community.

levee: an earth wall that prevents the flooding of a river.

lines of longitude: also called *meridians*; imaginary lines on the earth's surface, running from north to south poles. These lines are measured in degrees of longitude.

longitude: distance in degrees east and west of the prime, or zero, meridian.

luxury: something that gives pleasure or comfort, but is not essential to life and health.

medium of exchange: money.

merchant: a person who buys and sells goods for profit.

meridians: also called *lines of longitude*; imaginary lines on the earth's surface, running from north to south poles. Meridians are measured in degrees of longitude.

Mesopotamia: land between the Tigris and Euphrates rivers; now part of Iraq.

Middle East: region of the world where the two landmasses of Africa and Eurasia meet; often called the "cross roads" of the world.

millennium: 1,000 years (plural: millennia).

Mohenjo-Daro: one of the two known cities of the Indus River Valley civilization.

money: medium of exchange; anything generally accepted in exchange for other things.

mound: a "hill" formed of earth, sand, stone, bricks, etc., covering ruins. (See *tel*.)

natural environment: the land, climate, plants, and animals of an area.

necessity: something that a person needs to stay alive and healthy.

parallels of latitude: imaginary circles drawn east and west around the surface of the earth. The circles are the same distance from each other and grow smaller as they approach the poles.

patriotism: love of or devotion to one's country.

Persians: people who built a great empire in the Middle East about 525 B.C.

pharaoh: a ruler of ancient Egypt.

philosophy: a system of thought about the meaning of life and the nature of man.

physical environment: land and climate of an area. It includes the wild plants and animals.

poles: the two points at opposite ends of the earth's axis. They remain in a fixed position as the earth rotates.

political science: the scientific study of the principles and conduct of government.

politics: the day-to-day business of government; also, the struggle for power in or between governments.

priest-kings: the first rulers of Sumer; later replaced by military kings.

prime meridian: the meridian at 0° longitude. It is the point from which all degrees of longitude are measured east and west. The prime meridian runs through Greenwich, England.

property: things that are owned. Property may be owned by a person, a family, a group, or a government.

Queen Shubad: Sumerian ruler. Archaeologists made important discoveries about Sumer when they studied the contents of her grave.

rain-watered: description of land that has enough regular rainfall to grow crops without irrigation.

reference lines: on a globe, lines whose exact positions are known; used to locate places exactly. When reference lines cross they form a *grid*.

reference point: on a globe, a location whose exact position is known.

relief: in sculpture, a figure or design which stands out from the surface from which it was cut.

religion: belief in divine power; sometimes, men's beliefs about the nature of the universe and the purpose of life.

revolt: to rise up and use force against authority, such as government; to rebel.

revolution: (in politics) the result of a successful revolt; (in geography) the motion of the earth around the sun every 365¼ days. One revolution is called a year.

revolves: (in geography) moves in a circle around another body or object.

rotation: (in geography) the motion of the earth on its own axis every 24 hours. One rotation is called a day.

Sargon: king of the Akkadians who conquered Sumer.

shadoof: machine used to raise water, especially used in irrigation. It consists of a long rod with a bucket at one end and a weight at the other.

signature: a person's name or mark that he makes himself.

silt: earthy matter carried by moving or running water and deposited as soil.

skill: a craft, trade, or job that a person has learned to do well.

slave: a human being owned by another human being.

society: a group of persons living together as members of a community.

sociology: the scientific study of human society—how it developed, how it is organized, how it functions.

specialist: a person who devotes himself to one particular job.

Sumer: the land in southern Mesopotamia where the first civilization arose; now part of Iraq.

surplus: a quantity or amount of goods over and above what is needed to stay alive.

swamp: an area of wet, marshy ground; a marsh.

tax: a sum of money paid by people to the government for its support or for services.

tel: an artificial mound made up of the remains of a settlement or city of one or more ancient civilizations. (See mound.)

trade: an exchange of goods and money.

transport: to carry or move from one place to another.

Umma: a Sumerian city-state.

ummia: a school principal in Sumer.

Ur: the name of a Sumerian city.

ziggurat: a Sumerian hill temple, where the Sumerians worshipped their gods.

INDEX